UNDERSTAND ECONOMICS

BASIC CONCEPTS OF ECONOMIC SYSTEM

PREM AMRIT

Copyright © Prem Amrit
All Rights Reserved.

This book has been published with all efforts taken to make the material error-free after the consent of the author. However, the author and the publisher do not assume and hereby disclaim any liability to any party for any loss, damage, or disruption caused by errors or omissions, whether such errors or omissions result from negligence, accident, or any other cause.

While every effort has been made to avoid any mistake or omission, this publication is being sold on the condition and understanding that neither the author nor the publishers or printers would be liable in any manner to any person by reason of any mistake or omission in this publication or for any action taken or omitted to be taken or advice rendered or accepted on the basis of this work. For any defect in printing or binding the publishers will be liable only to replace the defective copy by another copy of this work then available.

Dedicated to my Family & friends.

Contents

Acknowledgements	vii
Copyright	ix
1. Understand Economics	1
2. Role And Economic Indicators	4
3. Gdp	6
4. Economic System	22
5. Macroeconomics	26
6. Microeconomics Vs. Macroeconomics	35
7. Finance And Economics	42
8. Inflation	43
9. Deflation, Disinflation And Devaluing	57
10. Money Supply	68
11. Economic Growth	75
12. Monetarism	79
13. Types Of Inflation	86
14. Weighted Average	104
15. Unemployment	124
16. Business Cycle	131
17. Behavioural Economics	137
18. Rational Choice Theory	141
19. Scarcity Or Deficit	148
20. Assumes Or Ceteris Paribus	153
21. Rational Person Or Rational Behavior	162
22. Heuristics	165

Contents

23. Anchoring And Adjustment	171
24. Game Theory	175
25. Economist	184
26. Positive Economics	187
27. Consumer Economics	196
28. Normative Economics	201

Acknowledgements

Thanks for everyone who support me and encourage me to write this book. Specially my family and friends. I thank for publishers who publish my book and thanks for readers who read my book.

Copyright

Copyright © 2022 Prem Amrit

This book has been published with all efforts taken to make the material error - free after the consent of the author. However, the author and the publisher do not assume and hereby disclaim any liability to any party for any loss, damage, or disruption caused by errors or omissions, whether such errors or omissions result from negligence, accident, or any other cause. While every effort has been made to avoid any mistake or omission, this publication is being sold on the condition and understanding that neither the author nor the publishers or printers would be liable in any manner to any person by reason of any mistake or omission in this publication or for any action taken or omitted to be taken or advice rendered or accepted on the basis of this work. For any defect in printing or binding, the publishers will be liable only to replace the defective copy by another copy of this work then available.

No part of this book may be reproduced, or stored in a retrieval system, or transmitted in any form or by any means, electronic, mechanical, photocopying, recording, or otherwise, without express written permission of the publisher.

COPYRIGHT

STOCKET LAB
Ganga Vihar Colony Makhdumpur
Digha Patna, Bihar.
https://linktr.ee/stocketlab
First published by Stocket Lab 2022
Copyright © Prem Amrit 2022
All Rights Reserved.
Cover design by: Prem Amrit

CHAPTER ONE

Understand economics

Assuming that people have unlimited needs in a world of limited means, economists analyse how resources are allocated to production, distribution, and consumption.

The study of microeconomics focuses on the choices of individuals and firms, while macroeconomics focuses on economic behaviour in general.

The global economy

As a business term, globalisation refers to the trend of international trade, investment, information technology, and outsourced manufacturing to weave together the economies of different countries. This is not a completely new concept – caravans have travelled everywhere since ancient times. Get valuable items like salt, spices, and gold to trade or sell in your country. Thanks to modern technology, globalisation unites the whole world with multinational corporations that produce, buy, and sell goods on a global scale. For example, a Japanese car company might manufacture auto parts in several developing countries, then ship those parts to another country for assembly, and then sell the finished car around the world. Globalisation is believed to help shift wealth to less developed countries as companies take advantage of lower labour and operating costs in developing countries, thereby creating jobs and economic benefits for the local economy. China is a good example of a country that has benefited greatly from globalisation. However, globalisation can be a double-edged sword. When national economies are intertwined, a recession in one country can overflow and affect the economies of other countries. Globalisation is also often blamed for job losses in developed countries as companies move manufacturing jobs overseas to cut costs.

One of the first recorded economists dates back to the 8th century BC. The Greek peasant and poet Hesiod wrote that in order to overcome shortages, it is necessary to distribute labour, materials, and time efficiently. Adam Smith's an Inquiry into the Nature and Causes of the Wealth of Nations, published in 1776, marked the beginning of modern Western economic theory.

Microeconomics

Microeconomics studies how individual consumers and companies make resource allocation decisions. Whether it is a person, a household, or a business, economists can analyse how these entities respond to price changes and why they ask them to do what they do at a certain price level.

Microeconomics analyzes how and why the prices of goods differ, how people make financial decisions, and how they trade, coordinate and cooperate.

In terms of the dynamics of supply and demand, the cost of producing goods and services, and how labour is allocated and distributed, microeconomics studies how businesses are organised and how people deal with uncertainty and risk in making decisions.

Macroeconomics

Macroeconomics is a branch of economics that studies the behaviour and performance of the entire economy. His main focus is on cyclical business cycles and broad economic growth and development.

The focus is on foreign trade, government fiscal and monetary policy, unemployment, inflation, interest rates, aggregate output growth, and business cycles that lead to booms, booms, recessions, and busts.

Economists use aggregates using macroeconomic models to help shape economic policy and strategy.

CHAPTER TWO

Role and Economic Indicators

What is the role of an economist?

Economists study the relationship between a society's resources and its production or output, and their opinions help shape economic policy related to interest rates, tax laws, employment programs, international trade agreements, and corporate strategies.

Economists analyse economic indicators, such as gross domestic product and consumer price indices, to determine major trends or make economic forecasts.

According to the US Bureau of Labour Statistics, 36 percent of US economists work for federal or state agencies. Economists also serve as professors in corporations or economic think tanks.

What are economic indicators?

Economic indicators detail the economic performance of a country. Economic indicators published regularly by government agencies or private organisations often have a significant impact on stocks, employment, and international markets, and often predict future economic conditions that will drive markets and guide investment decisions.

CHAPTER THREE

GDP

Gross domestic product (GDP):

Gross domestic product (GDP) is a macroeconomic indicator of the statistics of the national economy, expressing the total value of the final products of the sectors of material production and services produced in the territory of a given country.

GDP is one of the key indicators that quantitatively expresses the development of the economy.

It illustrates in the most general form how the economy grows and develops.

The reporting period is usually 1 year.

GDP is calculated in the national currency of a particular country and converted at the exchange rate.

At the same time, for a more correct comparison of the economic development of world states, it is often expressed in terms of purchasing power parity.

The structure of the GDP of each state is unique.

It depends on what part of the income brought in the reporting year to the state, for example, industry.

To determine the generalised level and speed of economic development, GDP per capita is used.

Gross domestic product (GDP) is the total monetary or market value of all industrial goods and services produced by a country in a given period. As a broad indicator of total domestic production, it serves as a comprehensive scorecard for a given country's economic health.

Although GDP is usually calculated on an annual basis, sometimes it is calculated on a quarterly basis. For example, in the United States, the government publishes annual GDP estimates for each fiscal quarter and calendar year. The individual datasets included in this report are in real terms, so the figures have been adjusted for price changes and therefore do not take into account inflation.

Gross domestic product is the monetary value of all manufactured goods and services produced by a country in a given period.

GDP provides an economic overview of a country and is used to estimate the size and growth rate of an economy.

GDP can be calculated in three ways: using expenditure, production, or income. It can be adjusted for inflation and population to provide a deeper understanding.

Real GDP takes into account the effects of inflation, but nominal GDP does not.

Despite its limitations, GDP is a key tool that guides policymakers, investors and businesses in making strategic decisions.

Understanding Gross Domestic Product (GDP)

The calculation of a country's GDP includes all private and public consumption, government spending, investment, increases in private stocks, paid construction costs, and foreign trade balance.

Of all the components that make up the country's GDP, the foreign trade balance is of particular importance. A country's GDP tends to increase when the total value of goods and services sold abroad by domestic producers exceeds the total value of foreign goods and services purchased by domestic consumers. When this happens, the country is said to have a trade surplus.

If the opposite happens—if domestic consumers spend more on foreign goods than domestic producers can sell to foreign consumers combined—this is called a trade deficit. In this case, the country's GDP tends to decrease.

GDP can be calculated in nominal or real terms, adjusted for inflation. In general, real GDP is the best way to express the long-term performance of a national economy because it uses constant dollars.

Suppose in 2012 the country's nominal GDP was $100 billion. Its nominal GDP will rise to $150 billion by 2022. Prices also rose by 100% over the same period. In this example, if you just look at its nominal GDP, the country's economy seems to be doing well. However, real GDP (in 2012 dollars) was only $75 billion, indicating a general decline in real economic performance over this period.

Types of GDP

GDP can be reported in several ways, each providing slightly different information.

Nominal GDP:

Nominal GDP is an estimate of economic production in an economy that includes current prices in its calculations. In other words, it does not rule out inflation or price increases, which could lead to inflated growth figures.

All goods and services included in nominal GDP are valued at the price of goods and services actually sold during the year. Nominal GDP is valued in local currency or US dollars at the exchange rate of the foreign exchange market in order to compare countries' GDP in purely financial terms.

Nominal GDP is used when comparing output in different quarters of the same year. When comparing GDP for two years or more, real GDP is used. This is due to the fact that, in fact, the effect of inflation is eliminated, which makes it possible to compare years only by number.

real GDP

Real GDP is an inflation-adjusted measure of the amount of goods and services an economy produces in a given year, with prices held constant each year to separate the effects of inflation or deflation from the evolution of output over time. Since GDP is based on the monetary value of goods and services, it is subject to inflation.

Rising prices tend to increase a country's GDP, but this does not necessarily reflect any change in the quantity or quality of goods and services produced. Therefore, looking only at a country's nominal GDP, it is difficult to say whether the increase in this indicator is due to the actual expansion of production or simply to higher prices.

Economists use the process of adjusting for inflation to get the real GDP of an economy. By adjusting output in any given year to the price level in the base year (called the base year), economists can adjust for the effect of inflation. So one can compare a country's GDP for a year to see if there has been real growth.

Real GDP is calculated using the GDP price deflator, which is the difference in prices between the current year and the base year. For example, if prices rose 5% from the base year, the deflator would be 1.05. Nominal GDP is divided by this deflator to get real GDP. Nominal GDP is usually higher than real GDP because inflation is usually positive.

Real GDP reflects changes in market values, thereby reducing the difference between annual output. If there is a large difference between a country's real GDP and nominal GDP, this could be an indication of severe inflation or deflation in its economy.

GDP per capita

GDP per capita is a measure of GDP per capita in a country. It shows that the output or per capita income of an economy can represent average productivity or average standard of living. GDP per capita can be expressed in nominal, real (inflation-adjusted), or purchasing power parity (PPP).

In its basic interpretation, GDP per capita shows how much economic output can be attributed to each citizen. It is also a measure of overall national wealth, as the market value of GDP per capita is also a simple measure of wealth.

GDP per capita is often analysed alongside more traditional measures of GDP. Economists use this measure to understand the domestic productivity of a country and other countries. GDP per capita takes into account the GDP and the population of the country. Therefore, it can be important to understand how each factor contributes to the overall outcome and impacts per capita GDP growth.

For example,

if a country's GDP per capita is growing at a stable population level, this may be the result of technological progress producing more at the same population level. Some countries may have a high GDP per capita but a small population, which usually means they have built a self-sufficient economy based on an abundance of specific resources.

GDP growth rate

The GDP growth rate compares the annual (or quarterly) change in a country's output to measure how fast an economy is growing. Usually expressed as a percentage, this measure is popular among economic policymakers because GDP growth is thought to be closely related to key policy targets such as inflation and unemployment.

If GDP growth accelerates, this could be a signal that the economy is overheating and the central bank may try to raise interest rates. Instead, central banks see declining (or negative) GDP growth (i.e., recessions) as a signal that interest rates need to be cut and that stimulus may be needed.

GDP at purchasing power parity (PPP)

While not a direct measure of GDP, economists look to purchasing power parity (PPP) to see how a country's GDP is measured in international dollars, adjusted for differences in local prices and the cost of living. And living standards are made.

Gross domestic product formula

GDP can be determined in three main ways. All three methods should give the same number when calculated correctly. These three methods are commonly referred to as the expenditure method, the output (or production) method, and the income method.

The expenditure approaches

The expenditure method, also known as the expenditure method, calculates the expenditures of the various groups involved in the economy. US GDP is primarily measured using the expenditure method. This method can be calculated using the following formula:

GDP = C + G + I + NX

Where

C = consumption;

G = government spending;

I = investment; and

NX = net exports

All of these activities contribute to a country's GDP. Consumption refers to personal consumption or consumer spending. Consumers spend money on goods and services such as groceries and haircuts. Consumer spending is the largest component of GDP, accounting for more than two-thirds of US GDP.

Thus, consumer confidence has a very important impact on economic growth. A high level of confidence indicates that consumers are willing to spend, while a low level of confidence reflects uncertainty about the future and a reluctance to spend.

Government spending refers to government spending on consumption and total investment. The government spends money on equipment, infrastructure and payroll.

When both consumer spending and business investment plummet, government spending can become more important than other components of a country's GDP. (This can happen, for example, after a recession.)

Investment refers to private domestic investment or capital expenditure. Businesses spend money to invest in their business activities. For example, a company may buy a car. Business investment is an important component of GDP because it increases the productive capacity of the economy and boosts employment.

The net export formula subtracts gross exports from gross imports (NX = exports - imports). Goods and services produced by an economy and exported to other countries, less imports purchased by domestic consumers, represent the country's net exports. This calculation includes all expenses of companies located in a given country, even if they are foreign companies.

Production (final) way or The Production (Output) Approach

The production method is essentially the opposite of the cost method. Instead of measuring the cost of resources that contribute to economic activity, the production method estimates the total cost of economic output and subtracts the cost of intermediate goods (such as the cost of materials and services) consumed in the process. The cost approach predicts the future in terms of costs, while the production approach looks back in terms of the completed state of economic activity.

The income approaches

The income approach is a middle ground between the other two approaches to calculating GDP. The income approach calculates the income from all factors of production in the economy, including wages paid to labor, land rent, interest returns on capital, and corporate profits.

For those items that are not considered payments to factors of production, the income approach makes some adjustments. On the one hand, there are certain taxes such as sales tax and property tax that are classified as indirect business taxes. In addition, depreciation is added to national income – reserves that enterprises set aside to replace equipment that is subject to wear and tear during operation. All this together constitutes the income of the country.

GDP vs. GNP vs. GNI

While GDP is a widely used metric, there are other ways to measure a country's economic growth. While GDP measures economic activity within a country's actual borders (regardless of whether the producers are domestic or foreign enterprises), gross national product (GNP) measures the total output of individuals or companies outside the country. The gross national product does not include the domestic production of foreigners.

Gross national income

(GNI) is another measure of economic growth. This is the sum of all incomes received by citizens or nationals of the country (regardless of whether the main economic activity is carried out at home or abroad). The relationship between GNP and GNI is similar to the relationship between the production (output) method and the income method used to calculate GDP.

GNP

uses the production method while GNI uses the income method. In GNI, a country's income is calculated as its domestic income plus its indirect business taxes and depreciation (and its net external income). Net income from foreign factors is calculated by subtracting all payments to foreign companies and individuals from all payments to domestic enterprises.

GDP adjustment

Some adjustments can be made to a country's GDP to make this number more useful. For economists, a country's GDP reflects the size of the economy, but provides little information about a country's standard of living. One reason for this is that population size and cost of living are not the same around the world.

Comparing China's nominal GDP with that of Ireland, for example, does not provide much meaningful information about the realities of life in these countries, since China's population is about 300 times larger than Ireland's.

To help with this, statisticians sometimes compare GDP per capita between countries. GDP per capita is calculated by dividing a country's gross domestic product by its population, and this figure is often used to gauge a country's standard of living. However, the measure is not ideal.

Assume that China's per capita GDP is $1,500 and Ireland's per capita GDP is $15,000. This does not necessarily mean that the average Irishman is 10 times taller than the average Chinese. GDP per capita does not tell the cost of living in a country.

Purchasing power parity attempts to solve this problem by comparing how much can be bought per unit of currency adjusted for currency in different countries - comparing the price of an item or package of items in two countries after adjusting for the exchange rate between the two countries. , in fact.

Purchasing power parity-adjusted real GDP per capita is a very accurate statistic for measuring real income, which is an important factor in wealth. A person in Ireland can earn $100,000 a year, while a person in China can earn $50,000 a year. In words, Irish workers live better. But if food, clothing and other items cost three times as much in Ireland per year as they do in China, Chinese workers actually earn more.

How to use GDP data

Most countries publish GDP data on a monthly and quarterly basis. In the United States, the Bureau of Economic Analysis (BEA) releases an interim quarterly GDP report four weeks after the end of the quarter, and a final report three months after the end of the quarter. BEA publishes rich, detailed content that enables economists and investors to gain information and insights on all aspects of the economy.

The impact of GDP on the market is generally limited as it is retrospective and a significant amount of time elapsed between the end of the quarter and the release of GDP data. However, if the actual figures are significantly different from expectations, the GDP performance may have an impact on the market.

Because GDP is a direct measure of economic health and growth, businesses can use GDP as a guideline for their business strategy. Government agencies such as the US Federal Reserve use growth rates and other GDP statistics as part of their decision-making process to determine what type of monetary policy to apply.

If growth slows, they may pursue an expansionary monetary policy to try to stimulate the economy. If growth is high, they can use monetary policy to slow growth and prevent inflation.

Real GDP is the best indicator of the health of an economy. It is widely watched and discussed by economists, analysts, investors and politicians. The early release of the latest data almost always has an impact on the market, although as mentioned above, this impact can be limited.

GDP and investment

Investors focus on GDP because it provides the basis for decision making. Corporate earnings and inventory data from GDP reports are an important resource for equity investors as both categories show overall growth over the period; The corporate earnings data also shows pre-tax profit, operating cash flow and a breakdown across all major sectors of the economy.

Comparing the GDP growth rates of different countries can play a role in asset allocation, helping to decide whether to invest in fast-growing economies abroad, and if so, in which ones.

An interesting metric that investors can use to understand the valuation of the stock market is the ratio of total market capitalization to GDP, expressed as a percentage. In terms of stock valuation, the closest thing to this is the ratio of a company's market capitalization to total sales (or revenue) measured per share, known as the price-to-sales ratio.

Just as stocks in different industries trade at vastly different price-to-sales ratios, the ratio of stock market capitalization to GDP is nearly the same across countries. For example, in 2020, the US market capitalization was 195% of GDP, compared to just over 83% in China and 1,769% in Hong Kong, according to the World Bank.

However, the purpose of this ratio is to compare it with the historical norms of a particular country. For example, at the end of 2006, the US market capitalization was 142% of GDP, but by the end of 2008 it had fallen to 79%. In hindsight, these are areas of serious overvaluation and undervaluation, respectively, of US equities.

The biggest shortcoming of the data is its lack of timeliness; investors only get one quarterly update, and revisions can be large enough to significantly change the percentage change in GDP.

History of GDP

The concept of GDP was first proposed in a report to the US Congress in 1937 in connection with the Great Depression, conceived and proposed by economist Simon Kuznets of the US National Bureau of Economic Research (NBER).

At that time, the main system of measurement was the gross national product. After the 1944 Bretton Woods conference, GDP was widely used as the standard measure of a national economy, however the United States continued to use GNP as the official measure of economic welfare until 1991 before moving to GDP.

However, beginning in the 1950s, some economists and politicians began to doubt the GDP. For example, some have observed that people tend to take GDP as an absolute measure of a country's failure or success, even though it does not take health, happiness, (inequality) and other components of social welfare into account. In other words, these critics draw attention to the difference between economic progress and social progress.

However, most pundits, such as Arthur Okun, an economist on President John F. Kennedy's Council of Economic Advisers, firmly believe that GDP is the absolute measure of economic success, arguing that for every increase in GDP there is a corresponding decrease in the unemployment rate.

Criticism of GDP

Of course, there are disadvantages to using GDP as an indicator. In addition to being untimely, GDP as an indicator has been criticized:

It ignores the value of informal or unregistered economic activity. GDP is based on recorded transactions and official data, so it does not take into account the extent of informal economic activity. GDP does not take into account the value of private employment, underground market activity or unpaid volunteer work, which can be of great importance in some countries, nor does it take into account the value of leisure time or home production, which are the prevailing conditions. Human life in all societies.

In a global open economy, it is geographically limited. GDP does not take into account the profits made in the country by foreign companies repatriated by foreign investors. This may overestimate a country's real output. For example, Ireland's GDP in 2020 is $426 billion and GNI is $324 billion, a difference of around $100 billion (or more than 20% of GDP), largely due to foreign companies in Ireland repatriating profits.

He emphasizes material returns without regard to general well-being. As mentioned above, GDP growth alone cannot measure the development of a country or the well-being of its citizens. For example, a country may experience rapid GDP growth, but this can come at a huge cost to society in terms of environmental impact and increased income inequality.

He ignores business activity. GDP takes into account only the production of the final product and new capital investment, and deliberately subtracts intermediate costs and transactions between firms. Thus, GDP overestimates the importance of consumption over production in an economy and is a less sensitive indicator of economic volatility than indicators that include business activity.

He views costs and waste as economic benefits. GDP views all final private and public spending as an increase in social income and output, whether or not it is actually productive or profitable. This means that apparently unproductive or even destructive activities are often seen as economic output and contribute to GDP growth. This includes, for example, expenditures used to generate or transfer wealth among members of society rather than to create it (such as administrative costs for taxes or funds for lobbying and rent-seeking); spending on investment projects demanded by consumers (such as building empty ghost towns or bridges that lead nowhere, are not connected to any road network); used to be inherently destructive or used only to compensate for other destructive activities rather than to create new ones Expenditure on goods and services of wealth (for example, in the production of weapons of war or in law enforcement and crime control measures).

CHAPTER FOUR

Economic system

The five economic systems illustrate the historical practice of allocating resources to meet individual and societal needs.

Primitivism:

In primitive agricultural societies, people produced household or tribal necessities by building dwellings, growing crops, and hunting.

Feudalism:

Feudalism was the political and economic system of Europe from the 9th to the 15th century, defined by lords who owned land and leased it to farmers for production, from whom they received promises of safety and security.

Capitalism:

With the advent of the Industrial Revolution, capitalism arose, which was defined as a production system in which business owners organise resources, including tools, workers, and raw materials, to produce goods for market consumption and profit. Supply and demand set market prices in such a way as to serve the best interests of society.

Socialism:

Socialism is a form of cooperative production. Economic socialism is a system of production in which private ownership of the means of production is limited or mixed. Price, profit and loss are not the decisive factors used to determine who is involved in production, what is produced and how.

Communism:

Communism believed that all economic activity was centralised through the coordination of state-supported central planners with joint ownership of production and distribution.

School of Economic Theory

Many economic theories evolve as societies and markets evolve and change. However, three disciplines of economics: neoclassicism, Keynesianism and Marxism have influenced modern society.

The principles of neoclassical economics are often used as the basis for illustrating the virtues of capitalism, including the tendency of market prices to equilibrate with changes in supply and demand. The best estimate of resources comes from the strength of individual desire and scarcity.

John Maynard Keynes developed Keynesian economics during the Great Depression. Keynes argued against neoclassical theory, showing that limited markets and government intervention in markets created a stable and fair economic system, and argued for monetary policy designed to boost demand and investor confidence during recessions.

Marxist economics is defined in Karl Marx's Capital. Marxist economics is a rejection of the classical view of economics against the idea of a free market, an economic system driven by supply and demand with little government control that benefits society. He argues that capitalism benefits only a few, while the ruling class gets richer by deriving value from the cheap labour provided by the working class.

What is a command economy?

A command economy is an economy in which production, investment, prices, and income are centrally determined by the government. A communist society has a command economy.

What is behavioral economics?

Behavioural economics combines psychology, judgement, decision-making, and economics to understand human behaviour.

Who has influenced economic research in the 21st century?

Since 2000, several economists have received the Nobel Prize in Economics, including David Card for his contributions to labour economics, Angus Deaton for his work on consumption, poverty and welfare, and Paul Krugman's analysis of trading patterns.

CHAPTER FIVE

Macroeconomics

What Is Macroeconomics?

Macroeconomics is the branch of economics that studies the behaviour of the economy as a whole—markets or other systems that operate on a large scale. Macroeconomics studies general economic phenomena such as inflation, price levels, economic growth rates, national income, gross domestic product (GDP), and changes in the unemployment rate.

It is a social science that studies the impact of incentives and decisions, specifically how incentives and decisions affect the use and allocation of resources. Microeconomics shows how and why different goods have different values, how people and firms can efficiently produce, exchange, and benefit from them, and how people can best coordinate and cooperate with each other. Generally speaking, microeconomics provides a more complete and detailed understanding than macroeconomics.

Some of the key questions that macroeconomics addresses include:

- What causes unemployment?

- What causes inflation?
- What creates or stimulates economic growth?

Macroeconomics attempts to measure how well an economy is performing, understand the driving forces, and predict how productivity will improve.

Macroeconomics deals with the efficiency, structure, and behaviour of the entire economy, while microeconomics is more concerned with the choices made by individual economic actors (e.g., people, households, industries, etc.).

Macroeconomics is the branch of economics that deals with the structure, performance, behaviour, and decision-making of the economy as a whole or as a whole.

The two main areas of macroeconomic research are long-term economic growth and short-term business cycles.

The modern form of macroeconomics is often defined as beginning with John Maynard Keynes and his theories of market behaviour and public policy in the 1930s; since then, several schools of thought have emerged.

Compared to macroeconomics, microeconomics focuses more on the influence and choices of individual actors (people, companies, industries, etc.) in the economy.

Microeconomics studies the decisions of individuals and companies about the allocation of resources for production, exchange, and consumption.

Microeconomics deals with prices and production in one market and the interactions between different markets, but leaves the study of aggregates on an economy-wide scale to macroeconomics.

Macroeconomists formulate various types of models based on logic and observed human behaviour, and test the models against real-life observations.

Understand macroeconomics

Microeconomics is the study of what can happen (trends) when people make choices in response to changes in incentives, prices, resources, and/or methods of production. Individual actors are often divided into microeconomic subgroups such as buyers, sellers, and business owners. These groups use currency and interest rates as a coordinated pricing mechanism to create supply and demand for resources.

There are two aspects to the study of economics: macroeconomics and microeconomics. As this term implies, macroeconomics considers the general macro-scenario of the economy. In a nutshell, he looks at how the economy as a whole behaves and then analyzes how the various sectors of the economy are related to each other to understand how the whole works. This includes looking at variables such as unemployment, GDP, and inflation. Macroeconomists develop models to explain the relationship between these factors. Governments use such macroeconomic models and the forecasts they generate to structure and evaluate economic, monetary and fiscal policies, corporations to strategize in domestic and global markets, and investors to forecast and plan the movement of various asset classes.

Given the sheer size of government budgets and the impact of economic policy on consumers and businesses, macroeconomics is clearly dealing with important issues. When applied correctly, economic theory can shed light on how the economy works and on the long-term consequences of specific policies and decisions. Macroeconomic theory can also help individual businesses and investors make better informed decisions by providing a better understanding of the impact of broad economic trends and policies on their industries.

Using Microeconomics

Microeconomics can be applied in a positive or normative sense. Positive microeconomics describes economic behaviour and explains what will happen if certain conditions change. Positive microeconomics suggests that consumers will be more inclined to buy less than they used to if manufacturers increase car prices. If a major copper mine in South America collapses, copper prices will rise as supply is limited. Positive microeconomics could help investors understand why Apple's stock could fall if consumers buy fewer iPhones. Microeconomics may also explain why a higher minimum wage might force Wendy's to hire fewer workers.

These interpretations, conclusions, and predictions of positive microeconomics can then also be normatively applied to dictate what individuals, businesses, and governments should do in order to obtain the most valuable or profitable model of production. Exchange, and consumption among market participants. Extending the meaning of microeconomics from what it is now to what it should be or what people should do also requires at least the implicit application of some ethical or moral theory or principle. Which usually implies some form of utilitarianism.

Limitations of Macroeconomics

It is also important to understand the limitations of economic theory. Theories are often created in a vacuum, missing certain real-world details such as taxes, regulation, and transaction costs. The real world is also very complex, including social preferences and issues of conscience that defy mathematical analysis.

Even if we limit ourselves to economic theory, it is important and appropriate to focus on key macroeconomic indicators such as GDP, inflation and unemployment. The performance of companies and their stocks are significantly affected by the economic conditions in which companies operate, and studying macroeconomic statistics can help investors make better decisions and identify turning points.

Similarly, it is invaluable to know which theories benefit and influence particular governments. The basic economic principles of a government will go a long way in how that government deals with taxation, regulation, public spending, and similar policies. By better understanding the economy and the impact of economic decisions, investors can at least get a sense of the possible future and act accordingly with confidence.

Microeconomic Methods

Historically, microeconomic research has been based on the theory of general equilibrium developed by Léon Walras in The Elements of Pure Economics (1874) and the theory of partial equilibrium presented by Alfred Marshall in The Principles of Economics (1890).

Marshall's method and Walras's method belong to a wide range of neoclassical microeconomics. Neoclassical economics focuses on how consumers and producers make rational choices in order to maximise their economic wealth, limited by how much income and resources they have. Neoclassical economists make simplifying assumptions about markets, such as complete knowledge, an infinite number of buyers and sellers, homogeneous goods, or static ratio variables, to construct mathematical models of economic behaviour.

These approaches attempt to represent human behaviour in a functional mathematical language, which allows economists to develop mathematically verifiable models of individual markets. Neoclassicism believes in making measurable assumptions about economic events and then using empirical evidence to see which assumptions work best. Thus, they follow the "logical positivism" or "logical empiricism" section of philosophy. Microeconomics applies a range of research methods depending on the problem being studied, and the behaviour associated with it.

Basic concepts of microeconomics

The study of microeconomics includes several key concepts, including (but not limited to):

Incentives and Behaviour: How people respond to situations they encounter as individuals or companies.

Utility Theory: Consumers will buy and consume combinations of goods that maximise their happiness or "utility", depending on how much income they can consume.

Production Theory: This is the study of production, or the process of converting inputs into outputs. Producers tend to choose resource combinations and combination methods that minimise costs to maximise profits.

Price theory: The interaction of utility theory and production gives rise to the theory of supply and demand, which determines prices in a competitive market. In a perfectly competitive market, it is concluded that consumers demand the same price offered by producers. This leads to economic equilibrium.

Area of macroeconomic research

Macroeconomics is a fairly broad field, but there are two specific research areas that are representative of this discipline. The first area defines long-term economic growth or increase in national income. The other concerns the causes and consequences of short-term fluctuations in national income and employment, also known as the business cycle.

The economic growth: Economic growth refers to an increase in the overall output of an economy. Macroeconomists seek to understand what promotes or hinders economic growth in order to support economic policies that support development, progress, and improved living standards.

Adam Smith's 18th-century classic, An Inquiry into the Nature and Causes of the Wealth of Nations, advocating free trade, laissez-faire economic policies, and an expanded division of labour is perhaps the first, and certainly the foundational one. Work in this research centre. By the 20th century, macroeconomists began to study growth using more formal mathematical models. Growth is often modelled as a function of physical capital, human capital, labour, and technology.

Business cycle: Superimposed on long-term macroeconomic growth trends, the levels, and rates of change in key macroeconomic variables such as employment and national product experience ups and downs, booms and busts from time to time, a phenomenon known as the business cycle. A notable recent example is the financial crisis of 2008, and the Great Depression of the 1930s was in fact the driving force behind the development of most modern macroeconomic theories.

History of macroeconomics

Although the term " macroeconomics" is not that old (it appeared in the 1940s), many of the main concepts of macroeconomics have been in the focus of research for much longer. Topics such as unemployment, prices, growth, and trade have been the focus of economists almost from the beginning of the discipline, although their research has become more focused and specialised in the 20th and 21st centuries. The early work of Adam Smith and John Stuart Mill, among others, dealt clearly with what is now considered the field of macroeconomics.

Macroeconomics in its modern form is often defined as beginning with John Maynard Keynes and his 1936 book The General Theory of Employment, Interest, and Money. Keynes provided an explanation for the effects of the Great Depression, when goods remained unsold and workers lost their jobs. Keynesian's theory tries to explain why markets may not clear up.

Prior to the popularization of Keynesian theory, economists generally did not distinguish between microeconomics and macroeconomics. As Leon Walras described, the same microeconomic laws of supply and demand that operate in individual product markets are understood as interactions between individual markets to bring the economy into general equilibrium. Economists such as Knut Wicksel, Irving Fischer, and Ludwig von Mises attribute the relationship between commodity markets and large-scale financial variables. Such as price levels and interest rates to the unique role that money plays as a medium of exchange in an economy.

Throughout the 20th century, Keynesian economics, as Keynesian theory is known, split into several other schools of thought.

CHAPTER SIX

MICROECONOMICS VS. MACROECONOMICS

Microeconomics vs. Macroeconomics: What's the Difference?

Macroeconomics is different from microeconomics, which focuses on the smaller factors that influence people's and companies' choices. The factors studied in microeconomics and macroeconomics often interact with each other. For example, the unemployment rate in an economy affects the supply of workers that a company can hire.

The key difference between microeconomics and macroeconomics is that macroeconomic aggregates can sometimes behave quite differently, even opposite, to similar microeconomic variables.

For example, Keynes cites the so-called thrift paradox, which argues that while saving may be the key to wealth accumulation for an individual. It can lead to a slowdown in economic growth, where everyone immediately tries to save more, reducing overall wealth in the process.

At the same time, microeconomics studies economic trends or what happens when people make certain choices. People are typically divided into subgroups such as buyers, sellers, and business owners. These actors interact according to the law of supply and demand for resources, using currency and interest rates as an agreed pricing mechanism.

Microeconomics vs Macroeconomics An Overview

Economics is divided into two broad categories: microeconomics and macroeconomics. Microeconomics studies individual and business decisions, while macroeconomics studies the decisions of countries and governments.

Although these two sectors of the economy look different, they are in fact interdependent and complement each other. There are many overlapping issues between these two areas.

Microeconomics studies individual and business decisions, while macroeconomics analyzes national and government decisions.

Microeconomics focuses on supply and demand and other factors that determine the price level, making it a bottom-up approach.

Macroeconomics takes a top-down approach, looking at the economy as a whole, trying to determine its process and nature.

Investors can use microeconomics in their investment decisions, while macroeconomics is an analytical tool mainly used to formulate economic and fiscal policies.

Microeconomics

Microeconomics is the study of the decisions that people and businesses make regarding the allocation of resources and the prices at which they trade goods and services. It takes into account taxes, regulations, and state laws.

Microeconomics focuses on supply and demand and other forces that determine the price level in an economy. It uses a bottom-up approach to economic analysis. In other words, microeconomics attempts to understand human choice, decision-making, and resource allocation.

Having said that, microeconomics does not attempt to answer or explain what forces should be at work in the market. Instead, he tries to explain what happens when certain conditions change.

For example, microeconomics studies how companies maximize output and capacity, thereby lowering prices and increasing competitiveness. A lot of microeconomic information can be gleaned from a company's financial statements.

Microeconomics includes several key principles, including (but not limited to):

Demand, supply, and equilibrium: prices are determined by the law of supply and demand. In a perfectly competitive market, suppliers offer the same prices as consumers. This creates an economic balance.

Production theory: This principle studies how goods and services are created or produced.

Cost of production: According to this theory, the price of a good or service depends on the cost of the resources used in the production process.

Labor Economics: This principle looks at workers and employers and seeks to understand patterns of wages, employment, and income.

The rules of microeconomics derive from a set of consistent laws and theorems, not from empirical research.

Macroeconomics

Macroeconomics, on the other hand, studies how a country's behavior and policies affect the economy as a whole. It analyzes entire industries and economies, not individuals or specific companies, so it is a top-down approach. It attempts to answer questions such as "What should the inflation rate be?" or "What stimulates economic growth?"

Macroeconomics analyzes how an increase or decrease in net exports affects a country's capital account, or how unemployment affects a country's gross domestic product (GDP).

Macroeconomics focuses on aggregates and econometric correlations, which is why governments and their agencies rely on macroeconomics when developing economic and fiscal policy. Investors buying interest rate sensitive securities should pay close attention to monetary and fiscal policy.

John Maynard Keynes is often considered the founder of macroeconomics, as he began to use monetary aggregates to study a wide range of phenomena. Some economists question his theory, while many Keynesian's disagree on how to interpret his work.

Investors and microeconomics and macroeconomics

Individual investors can better focus on microeconomics, but cannot completely ignore macroeconomics. Fundamental and value investors may disagree with technical investors about the proper role of economic analysis. While microeconomics are likely to affect individual investments, macroeconomic factors can affect the entire portfolio.

Warren Buffett once said that macroeconomic forecasts do not influence his investment decisions. Asked how he and his partner Charlie Munger decide to invest, Buffett said: "Charlie and I don't focus on macroeconomic forecasts. We've been working together for 54 years, and I can't remember a time when we invested in a stock or a company. We discussed macroeconomic issues."

Buffett also calls the macroeconomic literature "an interesting article."

Another famous and successful value investor, John Templeton, shares a similar view. "I never ask if the market is up or down because I don't know, and it doesn't matter," Templeton told Forbes in 1978. "I looked for stocks in country after country and asked: "Where is the lowest price compared to what I think they are worth?"

Will macroeconomic factors impact my portfolio?

Yes, macroeconomic factors can have a significant impact on your portfolio. For example, the Great Recession of 2008–2009 and the market crash that followed was caused by the bursting of the US housing bubble and the subsequent near-collapse of financial institutions that invested heavily in subprime US mortgages.

As another example of the impact of macro factors on a portfolio, consider the response of central banks and governments to the pandemic-induced collapse in the spring of 2020. The flood of liquidity released by governments and central banks through fiscal and monetary stimulus to strengthen their economies and stave off recession has sent most major stock markets to record highs in the second half of 2020 and much of 2021.

What is a global macro strategy?

A global macro strategy is an investment and trading strategy based on major macroeconomic events at the national or global level. " Global Macro" includes the study and analysis of numerous macroeconomic factors, including interest rates, currency levels, political events and relations between states.

- What is the fundamental difference between microeconomics and macroeconomics?
- Microeconomics is the study of how people and companies make decisions about the allocation of limited resources. Macroeconomics studies the economy as a whole.
- How do basic microeconomic concepts such as supply and demand affect stock prices?

Microeconomic concepts such as supply and demand impact stock prices in two ways: directly and indirectly.

The direct impact can be measured by the impact of supply and demand imbalances on share prices. When demand for a stock exceeds supply at a given point in time, because there are more buyers than sellers, stocks rise; conversely, when supply exceeds demand, inventory shrinks because there are more sellers than buyers.

Indirect effects are based on supply and demand for the products and services of the target company. If a company's product disappears from the shelves due to high demand, it could be on a strong earnings trajectory, which could lead to a higher share price. But if demand is low and there is excess inventory (or supply) of products, a company's profits can be disappointing and inventory can plummet.

Does the return of my portfolio depend on microeconomic and macroeconomic factors?

Yes, the performance of your portfolio depends on microeconomic and macroeconomic factors. Microeconomic factors such as supply and demand, taxes and regulation, as well as macroeconomic factors such as gross domestic product (GDP) growth, inflation, and interest rates have a big impact on various sectors of the economy and your investment portfolio.

CHAPTER SEVEN

FINANCE AND ECONOMICS

Economics and finance are interconnected, interact and influence each other. Investors care about economic data because it also influences the market to a great extent. It is important for investors to avoid" either-or" discussions about economics and finance; both are important and have the right to be applied.

Typically, the focus of economics, especially macroeconomics, is on the larger picture, such as country, region, or market performance. Economics can also focus on public policy, while finance is more focused on individuals, companies, or industries.

Microeconomics explains what happens if certain conditions change at the industry, company or individual level. If manufacturers raise car prices, microeconomics says consumers will tend to buy less than they used to. If a major copper mine in South America collapses, copper prices will rise as supply is limited.

Finance also focuses on how companies and investors value risk and reward. Historically, economics has been more theoretical and finance more practical, but over the past 20 years the difference has become less noticeable.

CHAPTER EIGHT

INFLATION

Inflation is an increase in prices, which can be translated as a decrease in purchasing power over time. The rate at which purchasing power is declining can be reflected in the increase in the average price of a basket of individual goods and services over a period of time. The price increase is usually expressed as a percentage, which means that the actual purchase of a unit of currency is lower than in the previous period. Inflation can be contrasted with deflation, which occurs when prices fall and purchasing power increases.

- Inflation is the rate at which the prices of goods and services rise.
- It is sometimes divided into three types: demand-pull inflation, cost-push inflation, and domestic inflation.
- The most commonly used inflation indices are the consumer price index and the wholesale price index.
- Inflation can be viewed positively or negatively, depending on personal views and the pace of change.

Those who own tangible assets, such as property or inventories of goods, may want to see some inflation as this increases the value of their assets.

Understanding Inflation

While it is easy to measure the change in the price of an individual product over time, human demand is not limited to just one or two products. People need a wide variety of products, as well as many services, to live a comfortable life. These include goods such as food, metals, fuels, utilities such as electricity and transportation, and services such as healthcare, recreation, and labor.

Inflation is designed to measure the overall impact of price changes on diversified products and services. It allows a single value to represent the increase in the price level of goods and services in an economy over a given period of time.

Prices are rising, which means that fewer goods and services are bought per unit of currency. This loss of purchasing power affects the cost of living for ordinary people, which ultimately leads to slower economic growth. Economists agree that persistent inflation occurs when a country's money supply grows faster than its economy grows.

To address this problem, monetary authorities (such as central banks) take the necessary measures to manage the money supply and credit to keep inflation within acceptable limits and keep the economy running smoothly.

In theory, monetarism is a popular theory that explains the relationship between inflation and the money supply in an economy. For example, after the conquest of the Aztec and Inca empires by Spain, a large amount of gold, especially silver, poured into the economy of Spain and other European countries.

As the money supply increases rapidly, the value of money falls, causing prices to rise rapidly.

Inflation is measured in several ways, depending on the type of goods and services. This is the opposite of deflation, which indicates a general decline in prices when inflation is below 0%. Remember that deflation should not be confused with deflation, a related term for a slowdown in (positive) inflation.

cause of inflation

An increase in the money supply is the main cause of inflation, although this can work through various mechanisms in the economy. Monetary authorities can increase the country's money supply by:

Print and give more money to citizens

Legal devaluation (devaluation) of fiat currency

Issuance of new funds as a reserve account loan through the banking system by purchasing government bonds from banks in the secondary market (the most common method)

In all these cases, the currency loses its purchasing power over time. The mechanisms by which it stimulates inflation can be divided into three types: demand-pull inflation, cost-push inflation, and domestic inflation.

Demand pull effect

Demand-pull inflation occurs when an increase in the supply of money and credit stimulates the aggregate demand for goods and services to grow faster than the economy can produce. This increases demand and causes prices to rise.

When people have more money, it leads to positive consumer sentiment. This, in turn, leads to higher payouts, which leads to higher prices. This creates a gap between supply and demand, where increased demand and less supply flexibility lead to higher prices.

Cost effect

Cost inflation is the result of rising prices for inputs in the production process. When the increased supply of money and credit is diverted to markets for goods or other assets, the value of various intermediate goods rises. This is especially true when the supply of key commodities is hit by a negative economic shock.

These changes lead to higher costs for finished goods or services and lead to higher consumer prices. For example, when the money supply increases, it causes a speculative boom in oil prices. This means that the cost of energy may rise and lead to higher consumer prices, which are reflected in various inflation measures.

Built-in inflation

Domestic inflation is related to adaptive expectations, or the idea that people expect the current rate of inflation to continue into the future. When the prices of goods and services rise, it can be expected that they will continue to rise at the same rate in the future. As a result, workers may demand more costs or wages to maintain their standard of living. An increase in their wages leads to an increase in the cost of goods and services, and this wage-price spiral continues as one factor causes another, and vice versa.

Types of price indices

Calculate and track a multi-item basket as a price index based on a selected set of goods and services. The most commonly used price indices are the consumer price index (CPI) and the wholesale price index (WPI).

Consumer Price Index (CPI)

The CPI is a weighted average of the prices of goods and services that measures the demand for a basket of key consumers. These include transportation, food, and healthcare.

The CPI is calculated by changing the price of each item in a predetermined basket of items and then averaging based on their relative weight in the basket. The price in question is the retail price of each item available for purchase by individual citizens.

CPI changes are used to estimate price changes associated with the cost of living, making it one of the most commonly used statistics to identify periods of inflation or deflation. In the United States, the Bureau of Labor Statistics (BLS) reports the CPI on a monthly basis and calculated it as early as 1913.

Wholesale Price Index (WPI)

WPI is another popular measure of inflation. It measures and tracks the price changes of commodities at various stages leading up to the retail level.

While WPI programs vary from country to country, they generally include programs at the manufacturer or wholesaler level. For example, this includes prices for raw cotton, cotton yarn, cotton blanks, cotton garments.

While many countries and organizations use the WPI, many others, including the United States, use a similar variant called the Producer Price Index (PPI).

Producer price index (PPI)

The PPI is a series of indices that measure the average change over time in the selling prices received by domestic producers of intermediate goods and services. PPI measures price changes from a seller's point of view, unlike CPI, which measures price changes from a buyer's point of view.

In all cases, an increase in the price of one ingredient (e.g., oil) may partially offset a decrease in the price of another ingredient (e.g., wheat). Collectively, each index represents the weighted average price change for that component, which can be applied to the economy as a whole, sector, or product level.

Formula for measuring inflation

A variant of the above price index can be used to calculate the amount of inflation between two specific months (or years). Although many ready-made inflation calculators are already available on various financial portals and websites, it is useful to know the basics to ensure accuracy and have a clear understanding of the calculations. Mathematically,

Inflation rate as a percentage = (ending CPI index / starting CPI) x 100

Let's say you want to know how the purchasing power of $10,000 changed between September 1975 and September

2018. Price index data can be found in tabular form on various portals. From this table, obtain the corresponding CPI data for the two months indicated. September 1975 was 54.6 (initial CPI) and September 2018 was 252.439 (final CPI).

Substitute in the formula to get:

Percent Inflation Rate = (252.439/54.6) x 100 = (4.6234) x 100 = 462.34%

Since you want to know how much $10,000 was worth in September 1975 in September 2018, multiply the inflation rate by that amount to get the modified dollar value:

Change in dollar value = 4.6234 x $10,000 = $46,234.25.

This means that $10,000 in September 1975 would be worth $46,234.25. Basically, if you purchased a $10,000 basket of goods and services (included in the CPI definition) in 1975, the same basket would cost you $46,234.25 in September 2018.

Advantages and Disadvantages of Inflation

Inflation can be interpreted as good or bad, depending on which side people are on and how fast the change is happening.

Advantage

Individuals who own tangible assets (such as property or inventory) that are valued in their home currency may want to see some inflation, as this raises the price of their assets, which they can sell for a higher price.

Inflation often causes businesses to speculate on risky projects, as well as people who invest in company shares, because they expect higher returns than inflation.

The optimum level of inflation is usually encouraged to stimulate spending to some extent rather than saving. If the purchasing power of money declines over time, there may be more incentive to spend now than to save and spend later. This can increase spending, thereby stimulating economic activity in the country. It is believed that a balanced approach allows keeping inflation values in the optimal and desired range.

Disadvantages

Buyers of such assets may be unhappy with inflation because they will have to pay more. People who own assets denominated in their own currency, such as cash or bonds, may not like inflation because it eats into the real value of their assets. As such, investors looking to protect their portfolios from inflation should consider inflation hedge asset classes such as gold, commodities, and real estate investment funds (REITs). Inflation-indexed bonds are another popular option for investors to profit from inflation.

High and erratic inflation rates can result in significant costs to the economy. Businesses, workers, and consumers must consider the impact of general price increases in their buying, selling and planning decisions. This creates an additional source of uncertainty for the economy, as their assumptions about future inflation rates may not be correct. It is expected that the time and resources spent on research, assessment, and adjustment of economic behavior will increase to the aggregate price level. This is contrary to real economic principles, which inevitably entail costs for the economy as a whole.

Even low, stable and easily predictable inflation rates, which some consider optimal, can cause serious problems for the economy. It has to do with how, where and when new money enters the economy. Whenever new money and credit enters the economy, it always ends up in the hands of a specific person or commercial company. The process of adjusting the price level of the new money supply occurs as they spend the new currency, which circulates from hand to hand and from account to account throughout the economy.

Inflation causes some prices to rise first and then others. This successive change in purchasing power and prices (called the Cantillon effect) means that the process of inflation does not simply raise the general price level over time. But it also distorts relative prices, wages, and profit rates in the process. Economists generally understand that deviations in relative prices from their economic equilibrium are harmful to the economy, and Austrian economists even consider this process to be the main driving force behind recession cycles.

Pros

- The result is a higher resale value of assets
- Optimal inflation stimulates spending

Cons

- Buyers should pay more for goods and services
- set higher prices for the economy

- Raise one price first, then another
- Controlling Inflation

A country's financial regulators have an important responsibility for controlling inflation. This is done through the implementation of monetary policy measures, which refers to the actions of a central bank or other committee to determine the money supply and growth rate.

In the US, the Fed's monetary policy goals include moderate long-term interest rates, price stability, and maximum employment. Each of these goals is designed to help create a stable financial environment. The Fed has clearly communicated its long-term inflation target to maintain a stable long-term inflation rate, which is considered good for the economy.

Price stability—or a relatively stable rate of inflation—allows businesses to plan for the future because they know what to expect. The Fed believes this maximizes employment, which is determined by non-monetary factors that fluctuate over time and are therefore subject to change. For this reason, the Fed does not set a specific goal for maximum employment, and much depends on the assessment of employers. Maximum employment does not mean zero unemployment because there will be some level of volatility at any given time as people leave and start new jobs.

Monetary authorities are also taking emergency measures in extreme economic conditions. For example, after the 2008 financial crisis, the Federal Reserve kept interest rates near zero and implemented a bond-buying program called quantitative easing (QE).

Some critics of the plan argued that it would jump-start dollar inflation, but inflation peaked in 2007 and declined steadily over the next eight years.

There are many reasons why QE did not lead to inflation or hyperinflation, the simplest explanation being that the recession itself was a very prominent deflationary environment and QE supported its impact.

As a result, US policymakers are trying to stabilize inflation at around 2 percent a year.

The European Central Bank (ECB) has also responded with aggressive quantitative easing to combat deflation in the euro area, with negative interest rates in some places. This is due to fears that deflation could spread throughout the eurozone and bring the economy to a halt.

In addition, countries with higher growth rates can absorb higher inflation rates. India is targeting around 4% (max 6% and min 2%) and Brazil is targeting 3.5% (max 5% and min 2%).

Hedge against inflation

Stocks are considered the best insurance against inflation because rising stock prices include the effects of inflation. Since almost all increases in the money supply in the modern economy are infusions of bank credit through the financial system, most of the direct impact on prices is in domestic currency-valued financial assets such as stocks.

There are special financial instruments that can be used to protect investments from inflation. These include Treasury Inflation Protected Securities (TIPS), which are low-risk, inflation-linked Treasury securities in which the principal amount of an investment is increased by a percentage of inflation.

There are also options for TIPS mutual funds or exchange-traded funds (ETFs) based on TIPS. To access stocks, ETFs, and other funds that help hedge against the dangers of inflation, you may need a brokerage account. Choosing a stockbroker can be a tedious process due to their diversity.

Gold is also considered a hedge against inflation, although this is not always the case in retrospect.

Extreme example of inflation

Since all currencies in the world are legal tender, the money supply can increase rapidly for political reasons, causing prices to rise rapidly. The most famous example is the hyperinflation that hit the German Weimar Republic in the early 1920s.

The country that won the First World War demanded reparations from Germany, but could not pay them with German paper money, as they were of dubious value due to government loans. Germany tried to print paper money, use it to buy foreign currency and use it to pay off debts.

This policy led to a rapid devaluation of the German mark and an accompanying hyperinflation. German consumers are responding to this cycle by spending their money as quickly as possible, knowing that the longer they wait, the less money they will be worth. More and more money is pouring into the economy, and its value has plummeted to the point where people are sticking almost worthless bills to the walls. Similar situations occurred in Peru in 1990 and Zimbabwe in 2007-2008.

What causes inflation?

There are three main causes of inflation: demand-pull inflation, cost-push inflation and domestic inflation.

Demand-pull inflation is a situation where insufficient production of a good or service to meet demand causes prices to rise.

On the other hand, cost-push inflation occurs when the cost of producing goods and services rises, forcing businesses to raise prices.

Domestic inflation (sometimes called the wage-price spiral) occurs when workers demand higher wages to keep up with rising costs of living. This, in turn, forces firms to raise prices to offset rising wage costs, leading to a self-reinforcing cycle of rising wages and prices.

Is inflation good or bad?

Too much inflation is generally considered bad for the economy, and too little inflation is considered bad. Many economists advocate low or moderate inflation of around 2 percent per year.

In general, higher inflation hurts savers because it reduces the purchasing power of the money they save. However, this can benefit borrowers as the inflation-adjusted value of their outstanding debt declines over time.

What is the impact of inflation?

Inflation can affect the economy in different ways. For example, if inflation causes a country's currency to depreciate, this can make goods priced in foreign currency more affordable, which benefits exporters.

On the other hand, this may lead to higher prices for foreign-made goods, which will harm importers. Higher inflation rates can also stimulate consumption, as consumers seek to buy goods quickly before prices rise even further. On the other hand, savers may see the real value of their savings depreciate, limiting their ability to spend or invest in the future.

Why is inflation so high now?

In 2022, inflation in the US and around the world will rise to levels not seen since the early 1980s. While there is no single reason for the rapid rise in world prices, a combination of events has caused inflation to reach such high levels.

The COVID-19 pandemic in early 2020 triggered lockdowns and other restrictive measures that dramatically disrupted global supply chains, from factory closures to seaport bottlenecks. At the same time, the government issued stimulus checks and increased unemployment benefits to help mitigate the financial impact of these measures on individuals and small businesses. As a COVID-19 vaccine became available, and the economy quickly recovered, demand (driven in part by stimulus money and low interest rates) quickly outstripped supply, with supply still struggling to return to pre-COVID levels.

Russia's unprovoked invasion of Ukraine in early 2022 resulted in a series of economic sanctions and trade restrictions on Russia, limiting global oil and gas supplies because Russia is a major producer of fossil fuels. Meanwhile, food prices have risen as Ukraine's incredible harvest cannot be exported. This led to similar growth further down the value chain as fuel and food prices rose.

CHAPTER NINE

DEFLATION, DISINFLATION AND DEVALUING

Deflation is a general decline in the prices of goods and services, usually associated with a reduction in the supply of money and credit in the economy. During deflation, the purchasing power of a currency increases over time.

Deflation is a general decline in the price level of goods and services.

Deflation is usually associated with a contraction in the supply of money and credit, but prices can also fall due to productivity gains and improved technology.

Whether the economy, price level, and money supply are deflationary or expanding, the attractiveness of different investment options is changing.

Understanding deflation

Deflation causes the nominal costs of capital, labor, goods, and services to fall, even though their relative prices may remain the same. Deflation has been a common problem among economists for decades. On the face of it, deflation benefits consumers because they can buy more goods and services for the same nominal income over time.

However, not everyone benefits from lower prices, and economists often worry about the impact of falling prices on various sectors of the economy, especially financial matters. In particular, deflation could hurt borrowers who may have to pay their debts with money that is worth more than they borrowed, as well as any financial market participants who invest or speculate on the prospect of higher prices.

Cause of deflation

By definition, monetary deflation can only be caused by a reduction in the supply of money or financial instruments that can be exchanged for money. In modern times, the money supply is most influenced by central banks such as the Federal Reserve. When the supply of money and credit decreases without a corresponding decrease in output, the prices of all goods fall. Periods of deflation most typically follow a long period of artificial monetary expansion. The early 1930s was the last time the United States experienced major deflation. The main reason for this period of deflation was the contraction of the money supply after the catastrophic bank failures. Other countries, such as Japan in the 1990s, have also seen deflation in recent times.

The world-famous economist Milton Friedman believes that with the optimal policy of central banks, striving for a deflationary rate equal to the real interest rate on government bonds. Nominal interest rates should be equal to zero, and the price level should steadily decline at real interest rates due to interest. His theory gave rise to

Friedman's rules, the rules of monetary policy.

However, falling prices can be caused by many other factors: falling aggregate demand (falling aggregate demand for goods and services) and rising labor productivity. A fall in aggregate demand usually leads to a subsequent fall in prices. Reasons for this shift include government spending cuts, the stock market crash, consumers' desire to save more, and monetary tightening (higher interest rates).

Price declines can also occur naturally when output grows faster than the supply of money and credit in circulation. This is especially true when technology improves economic productivity, and is often focused on products and industries that benefit from technological improvements. As technology advances, companies operate more efficiently. These operational improvements can reduce production costs and pass on cost savings to consumers in the form of lower prices. This is different from, but similar to, general price deflation, which is a general decline in the price level and an increase in the purchasing power of money.

Price deflation due to productivity gains varies across industries. For example, consider how productivity gains affect the technology sector. Over the past few decades, technological advances have led to a significant reduction in the average cost per gigabyte of data. In 1980, the average cost of 1 GB of data was $437,500, and by 2014 it was 3 cents. This decline led to a significant drop in the prices of goods produced using this technology.

Changing views on the impact of deflation

After the Great Recession, when currency deflation coincided with high unemployment and rising default rates, most economists viewed deflation as a bad thing. Since then, most central banks have adjusted monetary policy to promote a steady increase in the money supply, even though this encourages long-term price inflation and encourages debtors to over borrow.

British economist John Maynard Keynes warned against deflation because he believes that during a recession, when asset owners see their asset prices fall, deflation can bring down the cycle of economic pessimism, thereby reducing their willingness to invest. Economist Irving Fisher proposed a theory of economic depression based on debt deflation. Fischer argues that paying off debt after a negative economic shock leads to a greater reduction in the supply of credit in the economy. Which can lead to deflation, which in turn puts more pressure on debtors, leading to more liquidations and a spiral. Upset.

Recently, economists have increasingly challenged the old explanations for deflation, especially after a 2004 study by economists Andrew Atkeson and Patrick Kehoe. After studying 17 countries over a 180-year period, Atkeson and Kehoe found that 65 out of 73 deflationary episodes were not recessions, and 21 out of 29 depressions were not deflationary. It is now widely believed that deflation and price deflation are beneficial.

Deflation is transforming debt and equity financing

Deflation makes it less economical for governments, businesses, and consumers to use debt financing. However, deflation has strengthened the economic power of savings-based equity financing.

From an investor's perspective, companies that accumulate large cash reserves or have relatively little debt are more attractive in a deflationary environment. The opposite is true for businesses that are heavily indebted and have small cash reserves. Deflation also contributes to higher returns and increases the required risk premium for securities.

DISINFLATION

Deflation is a temporary slowdown in the rate of price inflation, and is used to describe a slight decrease in the rate of inflation over a short period of time.

Deflation is a temporary slowdown in the rate of price inflation, and is used to describe a slight decrease in the rate of inflation over a short period of time.

Unlike inflation and deflation, which refer to the direction of prices, deflation refers to the rate of change in the rate of inflation.

Moderate deflation is necessary because it prevents the economy from overheating.

The danger of deflation is that when inflation is as close to zero as it was in 2015, it creates the specter of deflation.

Understanding deflation

Deflation is often used by the Federal Reserve (Fed) to describe a period of slow inflation and should not be confused with deflation, which can hurt the economy. Unlike inflation and deflation, which refer to the direction of prices, deflation refers to the rate of change in the rate of inflation.

Deflation is not considered a problem because prices don't actually fall, and deflation doesn't usually signal the start of an economic downturn. Deflation is expressed as a negative growth rate, such as -1%, and deflation is expressed as a change in inflation, such as from 3% one year to 2% the next. Deflation is considered the opposite of reflation, which occurs when the government stimulates the economy by increasing the money supply.

Moderate deflation is necessary because it represents an economic downturn and prevents the economy from overheating. Thus, deflation is not unusual and is considered normal in good times for the economy. Deflation is beneficial to certain segments of the population, for example, those who seek to save their income.

Deflation trigger

Several things can lead to deflation in the economy. If the central bank decides to implement a tighter monetary policy and the government starts selling some securities, this could reduce the money supply in the economy, creating a deflationary effect.

Similarly, a contraction or recession in the business cycle can also trigger deflation. For example, firms may decide not to raise prices in order to gain more market share, leading to deflation.

Deflation since 1980

From 1980 to 2015, the US economy experienced one of the longest periods of deflation.

In the 1970s, a rapid rise in inflation known as the "Great Inflation" caused prices to rise by more than 110% in a decade. Annual inflation reached 14.76% in early 1980. Price increases slowed in the 1980s after the Federal Reserve implemented an aggressive monetary policy to reduce inflation, rising by only 59% over the same period. Prices rose 32% over the decade of the 1990s, followed by a 27% rise between 2000 and 2009 and a 9% rise between 2010 and 2015.

During periods of deflation, equities performed well, with an average real return between 1982 and 2015 of 8.65%. Deflation also caused the Federal Reserve to cut interest rates in the 2000s, causing bonds to generate above average returns.

The danger of deflation is that when inflation is as close to zero as it was in 2015, it creates the specter of deflation. Although inflation was close to zero in 2015, concerns about deflation have dissipated as it was largely due to falling energy prices. Inflation picked up as energy prices recovered between 2016 and 2020, averaging 1.8% over that period, and eased in 2020 due to the COVID-19 pandemic.

DEVALUING

Devaluation is a deliberate downward adjustment in the value of a national currency relative to another currency, currency group, or currency standard. Countries with a fixed or semi-fixed exchange rate use this monetary policy tool. It is often confused with devaluation, the opposite of revaluation, which refers to an adjustment in the exchange rate of a currency.

Devaluation is a deliberate downward adjustment in the value of a national currency.

The government that issued the currency decides to devalue the currency.

A weaker currency can lower a country's export costs and help reduce its trade deficit.

Learn about devaluation

The government of a country may decide to devalue its currency. Unlike depreciation, this is not the result of non-government activities.

One of the reasons a country can devalue its currency is to correct a trade imbalance. Devaluation lowers the cost of a country's exports, making it more competitive in the global market, which in turn increases the cost of imports. If import prices are higher, domestic consumers are less likely to buy, further strengthening domestic business. As exports increase and imports decrease, the balance of payments generally improves as the trade deficit narrows. In short, a country that devalues its currency can cut its deficit because there is more demand for cheaper exports.

Devaluation and currency wars

In 2010, Brazilian finance minister Guido Mantega warned of the possibility of a world currency war.

He used the term to describe the ongoing conflict between China and the US and other countries over the valuation of the yuan.

While some countries do not force their currencies to depreciate, their monetary and fiscal policies have the same effect, and they remain competitive in global trading markets. Monetary and fiscal policies with currency devaluation effects also stimulate investment by attracting foreign investors to assets such as the (cheaper) stock market.

On August 5, 2019, the People's Bank of China set the yuan's daily base rate below 7 for the first time in more than a decade. The move comes into effect on September 1, 2019, in

response to the Trump administration's new 10 percent tariffs on $300 billion worth of Chinese imports. There was a sell-off in global markets during this period, with the Dow Jones Industrial Average (DJIA) in the US down 2.9% on its worst day in 2019.

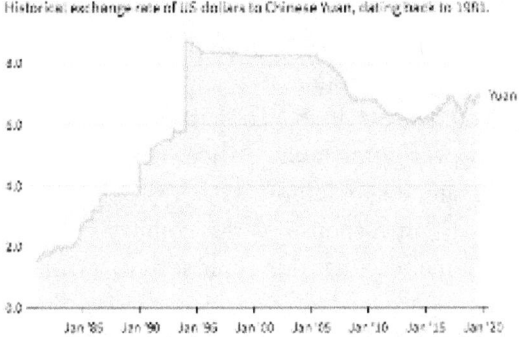

Chinese Yuan per US Dollar - Historical Chart

Historical exchange rate of US dollars to Chinese Yuan, dating back to 1981.

Source: https://www.macrotrends.net

In response, the Trump administration has labelled China a currency manipulator. This is just the latest wave of the US-China trade war, but certainly not China's first devaluation.

The reverse side or the downside of the devaluation

While currency devaluation can be an attractive option, it can have negative consequences. Raising import prices may protect domestic industry, but without competitive pressure it may be less effective.

Higher exports relative to imports can also increase aggregate demand, leading to higher gross domestic product (GDP) and inflation. Inflation may occur as imports become more expensive. Aggregate demand leads to demand inflation, and producers may not have an incentive to cut costs because exports are cheaper, which increases the cost of products and services over time.

Real world example

China has been accused of quietly devaluing its currency and trying to become a more dominant force in trading markets. Some accuse China of secretly devaluing their currency to revalue it after the 2016 presidential election and appear to be cooperating with the United States. However, after taking office, US President Donald Trump threatened to impose tariffs on cheaper Chinese goods, in part in response to the country's stance on its currency. Some fear that this could lead to a trade war and that China might consider a more aggressive alternative if the US follows suit.

President Trump has imposed restrictions on Chinese goods, including tariffs on more than $360 billion worth of imports. However, according to The New York Times, the 2020 COVID-19 pandemic has backfired. Global supply chains have not returned to the United States, and China's strong manufacturing position has solidified as consumers around the world have been locked down, staying at home and buying Chinese-made goods through e-commerce sites.

Egypt is under pressure from illegal market transactions in the US dollar, which began after a shortage of foreign exchange hurt domestic business and discouraged investment in the economy. In March 2016, the central bank devalued the Egyptian pound by 14% against the dollar to weaken the underground market.

According to a Brookings Institution article, the International Monetary Fund asked the pound to depreciate before allowing Egypt a $12 billion loan over three years. The Egyptian stock market reacted well to the devaluation. However, the illegal market reacted by devaluing the dollar against the Egyptian pound, forcing the central bank to take further action.

CHAPTER TEN

MONEY SUPPLY

The money supply is a measure of all the money and other moving instruments in a country's economy on that day. The money supply roughly includes cash and deposits, which can be used almost as easily as cash.

The government issues notes and coins through some combination of its central bank and treasury. Banking regulators influence the money supply available to the public by requiring banks to hold reserves, how they grant credit, and other monetary matters.

Money supply refers to the amount of cash or currency in circulation in an economy.

Various measures of the money supply also take into account non-cash items such as credit and loans.

Monetarists believe that, other things being equal, an increase in the money supply leads to inflation.

Understand money supply

Economists analyse the money supply and formulate policies around it by controlling interest rates and increasing or decreasing the amount of money flowing in the economy. Both the public and private sectors are analysed, as the money supply can affect price levels, inflation, and business cycles. In the United States, Fed policy is the most important determinant of the money supply. The money supply is also known as the money supply.

The impact of the money supply on the economy

An increase in the money supply generally lowers interest rates, which in turn stimulates consumption by increasing investment and putting more money into the hands of consumers. Businesses responded by ordering more raw materials and increasing production. The increase in business activity has increased the demand for labour. The opposite can happen if the money supply falls or its growth rates fall.

Changes in the money supply have long been recognized as a key driver of macroeconomic performance and business cycles. Schools of macroeconomics that primarily focus on the role of the money supply include Irving Fisher's quantity theory of money, monetarism, and Austrian business cycle theory.

Historically, the measurement of the money supply has shown the relationship between the money supply, inflation, and the price level. However, since 2000 these relationships have become unstable, which has reduced their reliability as a guide to monetary policy. Although money supply measures are still widely used, they are one of the vast amounts of economic data collected and analysed by economists and the Federal Reserve.

How to measure the money supply

The various types of currency in the money supply are generally classified as Ms according to the type and scale of the account in which the instrument is deposited, such as M0, M1, M2, and M3. Not all classifications are widely used, and each country may use its own classification. The money supply reflects the different types of liquidity for each currency in the economy.

For example,

M1, also known as narrow money, includes coins and banknotes in circulation and other cash equivalents that can be easily converted into cash. M2 includes M1, in addition to short-term deposits with banks and some money market funds. M3 includes M2 in addition to long-term deposits. However, M3 is no longer included in the Fed's report.

Money supply data is usually collected, recorded and published on a regular basis by national governments or central banks. The US Federal Reserve measures and publishes the total money supply M1 and M2 on a weekly and monthly basis. They can be found online or published in newspapers.

What happens when the Fed limits the money supply?

A country's money supply has a large impact on a country's macroeconomic conditions, especially as it relates to interest rates, inflation, and business cycles. In the United States, the Federal Reserve determines the level of the money supply. When the Fed restricts the money supply through tightening or hawkish monetary policy, interest rates rise and the cost of borrowing increases. This could ease inflationary pressures, but could also slow economic growth.

How is the money supply determined?

Central banks regulate the level of money supply in the country. Through monetary policy, central banks can take actions that follow expansion or contraction. Expansionary policies include increasing the money supply through measures such as open market operations, where the central bank uses a newly created currency to buy short-term government bonds, thereby putting the currency into circulation. Conversely, austerity would involve selling US Treasury bonds to get money out of the economy.

PRICE LEVEL

The price level is the average of the current prices of all goods and services produced in the economy. More generally, the price level refers to the price or value of a good, service, or security in an economy.

Price levels can be expressed in small ranges, such as a scale with the price of a security, or discrete values, such as dollar figures.

In economics, price levels are a key indicator closely monitored by economists. They play an important role in the purchasing power of consumers and the sale of goods and services. It also plays an important role in the supply and demand chain.

The price level is the average of the current prices of goods and services produced in the economy.

Price levels are expressed in small ranges or discrete values, such as dollar figures.

The price level is a leading indicator of the economy; an increase in prices indicates an increase in demand, leading to inflation, while a fall in prices indicates a decrease in demand or deflation.

In the investment world, price levels are called support and resistance levels, which help determine entry and exit points.

Understand price levels

In the business world, the term "price level" has two meanings.

The first is what most people are used to hearing: the price of goods and services, or the amount that consumers or other entities must give up in order to buy goods, services, or securities in the economy. Prices rise when demand increases and fall when demand decreases.

Price movements are used as a benchmark for inflation and deflation, or the rise and fall of prices in an economy. If the prices of goods and services rise too quickly when the economy is experiencing inflation, the central bank may step in and tighten monetary policy and raise interest rates. This, in turn, reduces the amount of money in the system, which reduces aggregate demand. If prices fall too quickly, the central bank can do the opposite: loosen monetary policy, thereby increasing the money supply and aggregate demand in the economy.

Another meaning of the price level refers to the price of assets traded in the market, such as stocks or bonds, and is often referred to as support and resistance. Just like price determination in economics, when the price of a security falls, the demand for it increases. This forms a support line. Selling occurs when prices rise, reducing demand. Here is the zone of resistance.

Price level in the economy

In economics, the price level refers to the purchasing power or inflation of money. In other words, economists describe the state of the economy by looking at how much people can buy with the same dollar. The most common price level index is the consumer price index (CPI).

Price levels are analysed using a basket-of-goods approach, in which the consumption bundle of goods and services is considered in aggregate. Changes in aggregate prices over time lead to an increase in the index that measures a basket of goods.

Usually, the weighted average is used instead of the geometric mean. Price levels provide a snapshot of prices at a given point in time, allowing you to view a wide range of price levels over time. Consumer demand for goods is also affected by rising prices (inflation) or falling prices (deflation), which leads to changes in broad measures of production such as gross domestic product (GDP).

The price level is one of the most closely monitored economic indicators in the world. Economists generally agree that prices should remain relatively stable from year to avoid excessive inflation. If the price level rises too quickly, the central bank or government will find ways to reduce the money supply or aggregate demand for goods and services.

Price levels in the investment world

Traders and investors make money by buying and selling securities. They buy and sell when the price reaches a certain level. These price levels are called support and resistance. Traders use these support and resistance areas to determine entry and exit points.

Support is a price level at which a downtrend is expected to stop due to concentrated demand. When the price of a security falls, demand for the stock increases, forming a support line. At the same time, the resistance zone arose due to sales when the price increased.

Once an area or zone of support or resistance is identified, it provides valuable potential trade entry or exit points. This is because when the price hits a support or resistance point, it does one of two things: it bounces off the support or resistance level, or it breaks the price level and continues in its direction until it hits the next support or resistance level.

CHAPTER ELEVEN

ECONOMIC GROWTH

Economic growth is the increase in the production of goods and services in an economy from one period to the next. It can be measured in nominal or real (inflation-adjusted) terms. Traditionally, overall economic growth has been measured in terms of gross national product (GNP) or gross domestic product (GDP), although alternative measures are sometimes used.

Economic growth is an increase in the production of goods and services in an economy.

Growth in capital goods, labour, technology, and human capital can fuel economic growth.

Economic growth is usually measured in terms of the increase in the total market value of additional goods and services produced using measures such as GDP.

Understand economic growth

Simply put, economic growth refers to an increase in the total output of an economy. Typically, but not necessarily, the total return to production is associated with an increase in average marginal productivity. This results in higher incomes and motivates consumers to open their wallets to buy more goods, which means a higher material quality of life or standard of living.

In economics, growth is often modelled as a function of physical capital, human capital, labour, and technology. In short, an increase in the quantity or quality of the working-age population, an increase in the tools they must use and the recipes they can use to combine labour, capital, and raw materials, will lead to an increase in output.

There are several ways to accelerate economic growth. First, it is an increase in the amount of physical capital goods in the economy. Adding capital to the economy tends to increase labour productivity. Newer, better, and additional tools mean that workers can produce more output in a given period of time. A simple example: a fisherman with a net catches more fish per hour than a fisherman with a sharp stick. However, two points are important for this process. Someone in the economy must first save in some form (through their current consumption) to free up resources to create new capital, and this new capital must be of the right type, in the right place, at the right time for workers to really make good use of it.

The second way to ensure economic growth is technological improvement. An example of this is the invention of gasoline fuel. Before gasoline was discovered as an energy source, the economic value of oil was relatively low. The use of gasoline is becoming a better and more efficient method of transporting work in progress and distributing the final product more efficiently. Improved technology allows workers to produce more output from the same stock of capital goods by combining them in new and more productive ways. Like capital gains, the pace of technological growth depends largely on the rate of savings and investment needed to participate in research and development.

Another way to ensure economic growth is to increase the labour force. Other things being equal, more workers produce more economic goods and services. Part of America's strong economic growth in the 19th century was due to the influx of cheap, productive immigrant labour. However, as with capital-driven growth, there are several key conditions in this process. Increasing the labour force also inevitably increases the amount of output that must be consumed to provide a basic standard of living for new workers, so new workers must be at least productive enough to make up for this and not become net consumers. Moreover, as with capital increases, it is essential to realise their productive potential that the right types of workers move to the right jobs in the right places, combined with the right types of complementary capital goods.

The last way is to increase human capital. This means workers become more proficient at their craft, increasing their productivity through skill learning, trial and error, or just more practice. Saving, investing, and specialising are the most consistent and manageable methods. In this context, human capital can also refer to social and institutional capital; behavioural trends that increase social trust and reciprocity, as well as political or economic innovations (such as improved protection of property rights) are actually types of human capital that can increase economic productivity.

Measured in dollars, not in goods and services

A growing or more productive economy produces more goods and provides more services than ever before.

However, some goods and services are considered more valuable than others. For example, a smartphone is considered more valuable than a pair of socks. Growth must be measured by the value of goods and services, not just their quantity.

Another problem is that not everyone values the same goods and services in the same way. Heaters are more valuable to Alaskans, while air conditioners are more valuable to Florida residents. Some people value steak more than fish, and vice versa. Since value is subjective, it is difficult to measure it for everyone.

CHAPTER TWELVE

MONETARISM

Monetarism is a macroeconomic theory that states that governments can promote economic stability by controlling the growth rate of the money supply. Essentially, it is a set of views based on the idea that the total amount of money in an economy is the main determinant of economic growth.

Monetarism is a macroeconomic theory that states that governments can promote economic stability by controlling the growth rate of the money supply.

Monetarism is based on the quantity theory of money, which states that the money supply (M) multiplied by the annual rate of spending (V) equals nominal spending (P × Q) in the economy.

Monetarism is closely related to the economist Milton Friedman, who believes that the government should keep the money supply fairly stable, increasing it slightly each year, mainly so that the economy can grow naturally.

Monetarism is a branch of Keynesian economics that emphasises the use of monetary policy rather than fiscal policy to manage aggregate demand, in contrast to much of Keynesianism.

While most modern economists reject the emphasis on monetary growth that monetarists have made in the past, some of the basic tenets of the theory have become the basis of non-monetary analysis.

Understand monetarism

Monetarism is an economic school that asserts that the money supply in the economy is the main engine of economic growth. As the amount of money available in the system increases, the aggregate demand for goods and services increases. An increase in aggregate demand stimulates job creation, which reduces unemployment and stimulates economic growth.

Monetary policy is an economic instrument used in monetarism to regulate interest rates and thus control the money supply. When interest rates rise, people are more motivated to save than to spend by shrinking or shrinking the money supply. Conversely, when interest rates are lowered with an expansionary monetary program, the cost of borrowing goes down, meaning people can borrow more and spend more, stimulating the economy.

Milton Friedman and monetarism

Monetarism is closely related to the economist Milton Friedman, who argued that, based on the quantity theory of money, the government should keep the money supply fairly stable, increasing it slightly each year to allow the economy to grow naturally. Because of the possible inflationary consequences of an excessive expansion of the money supply, Friedman. Who put forward the theory of monetarism, advocated that monetary policy should be aimed at the growth rate of the money supply in order to maintain economic and price stability?

Friedman, in his book A Monetary History of the United States 1867-1960, proposed a fixed growth rate known as the K percentage rule. Arguing that the money supply should grow at a constant rate related to nominal annual gross domestic product (GDP) growth. Growth rate) and is expressed as a fixed percentage each year. Thus, the money supply is expected to grow moderately, businesses will be able to forecast changes in the money supply each year and plan accordingly, the economy will grow steadily and inflation will remain low.

Quantity theory of money

Monetarism is based on the " quantity theory of money", which monetarists adopted from earlier economic theory and included in the general Keynesian structure of macroeconomics. The quantity theory of money can be summarised as the equation of exchange, formulated by John Stuart Mill, which states that the money supply multiplied by the annual rate of money spending is equal to the nominal spending in the economy. The formula looks like this:

$MV = PQ$

where:

M=money supply

V=velocity (rate at which money changes hands)

P=average price of a good or service

Q=quantity of goods and services sold

The key point to note is that monetarists see changes in M (money supply) as the driving force behind the equation. In short, changes in M directly affect and determine employment, inflation (P) and production (Q). In the original version of the quantity theory of money, V was assumed to be constant, but John Maynard Keynes abandoned this assumption, and the monetarists instead did not assume that V was easy to predict.

Economic growth is a function of economic activity (Q) and inflation (P). If V is constant (or at least predictable), then increasing (or decreasing) M will increase (or decrease) P or Q.

An increase in P means that Q will remain constant, and an increase in Q means that P will be relatively constant. According to monetarism, changes in the money supply will impact the long-term price level and short-term output. Therefore, changes in the money supply will directly determine prices, production, and employment.

Monetarism and Keynesian economics

The idea that speed is constant was a source of controversy among Keynesians, who argued that speed should not be constant because the economy is unstable and subject to cyclical instability. Conversely, the Keynesian theory of liquidity preference emphasises how changes in the demand for money (and hence in the velocity of circulation) impact the price level and aggregate demand.

Monetarism builds on Keynesian theory, assuming the same macroeconomic framework and integrating the equations of exchange (V oscillates cyclically, as Keynes said), but instead focuses on the role played by the money supply. Because they believe that V can be predicted relatively easily, monetarists believe that the equation of exchange can be resurrected as a method of stabilising policy, and they advocate using monetary policy to do so.

Supporters of monetarism generally believe that controlling the economy through fiscal policy is a bad decision, since it will inevitably lead to microeconomic distortions that reduce economic efficiency. They prefer monetary policy as an aggregate demand management tool that is more micro-economically neutral and avoids the dead weight and social costs of fiscal policy in the market.

History of monetarism

Monetarism rose to prominence in the 1970s, a decade marked by high and rising inflation and slow economic growth. Monetary policy has been responsible for lowering inflation in the US and UK. After US inflation peaked at 20% in 1979, the Fed changed its operating strategy to reflect monetarism. During this period, economists, governments, and investors avidly followed every new money supply statistic.

However, in the following years, monetarism fell out of favour with many economists, as it turned out that the relationship between various measures of the money supply and inflation was not as clear-cut as most monetarist theories assumed. Moreover, in subsequent decades, the ability of monetarism to explain the US economy has diminished. Today, many central banks have stopped setting monetary policy targets and instead set strict inflation targets.

While most modern economists reject the emphasis on monetary growth that monetarists have made in the past, some basic tenets of the theory have become the basis of non-monetary analysis. The most important of these ideas is that inflation cannot continue indefinitely without an increase in the money supply. In addition, controlling inflation is the responsibility of the central bank (although not the main task).

At the same time, the monetarist interpretation of the economic events of the past is still relevant today. Former Federal Reserve Chairman Ben Bernanke cited Friedman's work when he decided to lower interest rates and increase the US money supply to stimulate the economy during the global recession that began in the United States in 2007.

Real-world examples of monetarism

In Friedman's seminal book A Monetary History of the United States, 1867–1960–1930, co-authored with economist Anna Schwartz. According to Friedman and Schwartz, the Fed failed to ease the downward pressure on the money supply and ended up doing the opposite of what they should have done by shrinking the money supply. According to Friedman and Schwartz, the market tends to be the centre of stability; if the money supply is not set properly, the market will behave abnormally.

When Paul Volcker became chairman of the Fed in 1979, he made fighting inflation a top priority for the central bank. As suggested by Friedman and Schwartz, Volker limited the money supply for this. In 1980, he raised the federal funds rate to 20%. So far, this strategy against stagflation (high inflation combined with high unemployment and stagnant demand) has been successful. Volcker's policies reduced the money supply, consumers stopped buying, and businesses stopped raising prices. However, while this led to a huge fall in inflation, it did lead to the Great Recession (the 1980-82 recession).

During the same period, the UK was also struggling with severe inflation. When Margaret Thatcher was elected prime minister in 1979, she also introduced a series of monetary measures to combat rising prices in the country.

By 1983, inflation in the UK had halved, from 10% to 5%.

However, the popularity of monetarism was relatively short-lived. In the 1980s and 1990s, the link between the money supply and nominal GDP broke down, the quantity theory of money—the basis of monetarism—was questioned, and many of the economists who recommended monetarism in the 1970s abandoned the method.

CHAPTER THIRTEEN

TYPES OF INFLATION

DEMAND-PULL INFLATION

Demand-pull inflation is upward pressure on prices following a shortage of supply, a situation that economists describe as "too many dollars chasing too few goods".

When demand exceeds supply, prices rise. This is demand-pull inflation.

In general, low unemployment is no doubt a good thing, but it leads to inflation because more people have more disposable income.

An increase in government spending is also good for the economy, but can lead to shortages of certain goods and subsequent inflation.

Understanding Demand Inflation

The term demand-pull inflation usually describes a general phenomenon. That is, demand-pull inflation occurs when consumer demand exceeds the available supply of many consumer goods, resulting in an overall increase in the cost of living.

Demand-pull inflation is a principle of Keynesian economics that describes the consequences of an imbalance between aggregate demand and supply. When aggregate demand in an economy greatly exceeds aggregate supply, prices rise. This is the most common cause of inflation.

In Keynesian economics, an increase in employment leads to an increase in aggregate demand for consumer goods. In response to demand, companies are hiring more people to increase production. The more people a company hires, the more employment increases. Ultimately, the demand for consumer goods exceeds the ability of manufacturers to supply.

There are five causes of demand inflation:

Growing economy:

When consumers feel confident, they spend more and take on more debt. This leads to a steady increase in demand, and hence higher prices.

Increase in export demand: A sudden rise in exports causes the base currency to depreciate.

Government spending:

When government spending is more liberal, prices rise.

Inflation Expectations:

Companies may raise prices in anticipation of inflation in the near future.

More money in the system:

The expansion of the money supply causes there to be too few items that cannot be bought, causing prices to rise.

Demand inflation versus cost inflation

Cost-push inflation occurs when money moves from one sector of the economy to another. In particular, rising production costs such as raw materials and wages are inevitably passed on to consumers in the form of higher prices for finished products.

Demand-pull inflation and cost-push inflation actually move in the same way, but they affect different aspects of the system. Demand-pull inflation shows why prices are rising. Cost-push inflation shows that once inflation has started, it is difficult to stop it.

Demand inflation example

Suppose the economy is in a boom period and the unemployment rate falls to a new low. Interest rates are also low. To keep more gas-guzzling cars on the road, the federal government is offering a special tax credit for people who buy fuel-efficient cars. The big car companies were excited, though they didn't expect such optimism to coincide.

Demand for many models has skyrocketed, but manufacturers really can't get them fast enough. The prices of the most popular models have risen, and discounts are rare. The result is an increase in the average price of new cars.

However, not only cars were impacted. Because almost everyone has a paid job and low interest rates on loans, consumers are spending more on many products than is available. This is demand-pull inflation.

COST-PUSH INFLATION

Cost-push inflation (also known as wage-push inflation) occurs when overall prices rise (inflation) due to increases in wages and raw material costs. Higher production costs reduce the total supply (total production) in the economy. Since the demand for the commodity has not changed, the price increase of production is passed on to the consumer, creating cost-push inflation.

Cost-push inflation can be compared to demand-pull inflation.

Cost-push inflation occurs when overall prices rise (inflation) due to increases in wages and raw material costs.

Cost-push inflation occurs when higher production costs reduce the aggregate supply (total production) in the economy.

Since the demand for the commodity has not changed, the price increase of production is passed on to the consumer, creating cost-push inflation.

Understanding Cost-Push Inflation

Inflation is a measure of how fast the prices of a selected basket of goods and services in an economy are rising. If wages don't grow enough or keep pace with price increases, inflation can eat into consumers' purchasing power. If a company's production costs rise, the company's executive management may try to pass the extra cost on to consumers by raising product prices. If the company does not raise prices, and the cost of production increases, the company's profits will decrease.

The most common cause of cost-push inflation starts with an increase in production costs, which may or may not be expected. For example, the cost of raw materials or inventory used in production may increase, leading to higher costs.

In order for cost-push inflation to occur, demand for affected products must remain constant during periods of change in production costs. To cover increased production costs, producers raise prices to consumers to maintain profit levels while keeping pace with expected demand.

Reasons for Cost-Push Inflation

As mentioned earlier, the cost of inputs used in manufacturing increases, such as raw materials. For example, if a company uses copper in its manufacturing process and the price of the metal suddenly rises, the company may pass on these increased costs to their customers.

An increase in labour costs can create cost-push inflation, for example by mandating increases in the wages of production employees due to an increase in the minimum wage per worker. Worker strikes due to stalled contract negotiations can also lead to lower production; as a result, higher prices.

Unexpected causes of cost-push inflation are often natural disasters, including floods, earthquakes, fires, or tornadoes. If a catastrophe causes unexpected damage to a production facility and shuts down or partially disrupts the production chain, higher production costs may follow. A company may have no choice but to raise prices to help cover some of the damage caused by the disaster. Although not all natural disasters result in higher production costs, and therefore do not lead to cost-push inflation.

It may qualify if other events result in higher production costs, such as a sudden change of government that affects the country's ability to maintain its previous output. However, government-induced increases in production costs are more common in developing countries.

Changes in government regulations and existing laws, although generally expected, can lead to higher costs for businesses because they cannot compensate for the increased costs associated with them. For example, the government may require health care, driving up the cost of employees or labour.

Cost Push vs Demand Pull

The increase in prices caused by consumers wanting more goods is called demand-pull inflation. Demand-pull inflation includes periods when demand grows so much that production cannot keep up, which usually leads to higher prices. Simply put, cost-push inflation is driven by supply costs, while demand-pull inflation is driven by consumer demand — both result in higher prices being passed on to consumers.

An example of cost-push inflation

The Organisation of the Petroleum Exporting Countries (OPEC) is a cartel of 13 member countries that produce and export oil. In the early 1970s, OPEC imposed an oil embargo on the United States and other countries due to geopolitical events. OPEC banned oil exports to target countries and imposed production cuts. A supply shock ensued, with oil prices quadrupling from around $3 a barrel to $12. Cost-push inflation ensues as the demand for goods does not increase. The impact of supply cuts has led to soaring natural gas prices and higher production costs for companies that use petroleum products.

What causes inflation?

There are several reasons for what is considered inflation or a general increase in prices, and the exact reason is still debated among economists. The theory of monetarism argues that the money supply is the main cause of inflation and that the more money in the economy, the higher prices. Cost-push inflation theory states that because factors such as rising wages result in higher costs for producers, these higher costs are passed on to consumers. Demand-pull inflation refers to an increase in prices when aggregate demand continually exceeds the supply of available goods.

Is inflation always bad?

In theory, low inflation could be a good sign of economic growth. However, high inflation can be devastating (as can deflation or falling prices). Note that inflation is not always bad for certain groups of people. For example, fixed-rate borrowers tend to benefit from inflation while lenders and savers suffer.

What is a wage price spiral?

The wage-price spiral is a view of cost-push inflation, the belief that rising wages create more demand, which leads to higher prices. Thus, these higher prices induce workers to demand higher wages, and the cycle repeats.

CONSUMER PRICE INDEX (CPI)

The composite measure used to assess price changes for a basket of goods and services that reflects consumer spending in an economy is called the consumer price index.

The consumer price index (CPI) is a measure of the general price level in an economy. The CPI consists of a basket of commonly bought goods and services. The CPI measures changes in the purchasing power of a country's currency as well as the price level of a basket of goods and services.

The market basket used to calculate the CPI represents consumer spending in the economy and is a weighted average of the prices of goods and services.

Calculate consumer price index

The CPI reflects the change in the current price of a basket of goods over a period compared to the base period. The CPI is usually calculated monthly or quarterly. It is based on a representative expenditure pattern of city dwellers, including people of all ages.

The calculations involved in estimating the CPI are very strict. The consumption items are classified and different categories and subcategories are formed based on consumption categories such as urban or rural. Based on these derived indices and sub-indices, the final composite price index is mainly calculated by the national statistical agency. It is one of the most important economic statistics and is usually based on a weighted average of commodity prices. This gives an idea of the cost of living.

Inflation is measured using the CPI. The percentage change in this index over a given period of time gives a measure of inflation, the increase in prices for a representative basket of goods consumed over that particular period.

The CPI is one of the most popular measures of inflation and deflation. The CPI report uses a different survey methodology, price sample, and index weight than the Producer Price Index (CPI), which measures price changes.

Use of the consumer price index

As an economic indicator, the consumer price index is a measure of the inflation experienced by end users. It can determine the purchasing power of the dollar. It is also an indicator of the effectiveness of the state economic policy.

Adjusting other economic indicators for price changes: for example, the CPI can be used to adjust components of national income.

Provides a cost-of-living adjustment for the working class and Social Security recipients and prevents inflation-driven tax increases.

CPI limits

The CPI may not apply to all groups of people. For example, the CPI-U (urban) better reflects the US urban population, but does not reflect the rural population.

The CPI does not provide official estimates for subgroups of the population.

The CPI is a notional measure of the cost of living and does not measure all aspects that affect living standards.

These two fields cannot be compared. A higher index in one area than another does not always mean higher prices in that area.

Social and environmental factors go beyond the definition of the index.

CPI measurement limitations

Sampling error:

The risk of choosing the wrong sample. The selected sample may not accurately reflect the entire population.

Non-sampling errors:

Non-sampling errors include errors related to the collection of price data and errors related to operational implementation.

Excluding Energy

Costs: The main criticism of the CPI is that it excludes energy costs, even though they are a major expense for most households.

WHOLESALE PRICE INDEX (WPI)

The Wholesale Price Index is the price of a basket of wholesale goods. WPI focuses on the prices of goods that companies trade. It doesn't focus on what consumers buy.

The main purpose of the WPI is to monitor price fluctuations that reflect supply and demand in manufacturing, construction, and industry.

WPI helps assess the macroeconomic and microeconomic conditions of an economy.

The Importance of the HUD

In a dynamic world, prices don't stay the same.

The inflation rate, calculated on the basis of the dynamics of the wholesale price index (WPI), is an important indicator for tracking price developments.

Because it captures price movements in the most complete way, WPI is widely used by governments, banks, industry, and businesses.

Significant changes in monetary and fiscal policy are often associated with changes in the WPI.

Similarly, the movement of the WPI is an influential factor when the government of India formulates trade, fiscal and other economic policies.

The WPI is also used in terms of upgrading the supply of raw materials, machinery, and construction work.

WPI is used as a deflator for various nominal macroeconomic variables, including gross domestic product (GDP).

Wholesale Price Index (WPI)

Typically, WPI and CPI (Consumer Price Index) are used to calculate the rate of inflation. In India, the inflation rate is based on the WPI published by the Department of Trade and Industry.

The CPI is a measure of the weighted average price of a set of consumer goods and services purchased by households, such as transport, food, and health care.

India experienced its highest inflation rate of 34.68% in September 1974. The lowest inflation rate was -11.31% in May 1976.

How the Wholesale Price Index (WPI) works?

The wholesale price index is released monthly to track the overall rate of change in producer and wholesale prices. The index has a base period of 100 and is calculated based on subsequent price changes in the total output of goods.

To illustrate, let's take January 2021 as the base period. If next year the aggregate price level rises by 9.7%, then the WPI index in January 2022 will reach 109.7.

The WPI usually considers commodity prices, but the products included vary by country. They can also be changed as needed to better reflect the current economy. Some smaller countries only compare prices for 100-200 items, while larger countries tend to include thousands of items in their WPI.

PURCHASING POWER

The purchasing power of the average per capita cash income of the population reflects the potential of the population in the acquisition of goods and services, expressed in the commodity equivalent of the average monthly cash income of the population. A commodity equivalent is understood as the quantity of any one product (service) with certain consumer properties, which can be purchased provided that all cash receipts are used only for these purposes. The calculation is based on: the value of the monthly average per capita monetary income of the population and the average consumer price of products (services)—representative data registered in the consumer market. The indicator is calculated on an accrual basis from the beginning of the year.

Purchasing power is the value of a currency, expressed as the amount of goods or services that can be purchased with one unit of currency. Over time, it will weaken due to inflation. This is because raising prices actually reduces the amount of goods or services you can buy. Purchasing power is also known as the purchasing power of money.

In terms of investment, purchasing power or purchasing power is the amount of credit available to a client based on the existing bank securities in the client's brokerage account.

Purchasing power

Inflation reduces the purchasing power of a currency and what can be bought with that currency. The loss of purchasing power leads to higher prices. To measure purchasing power in the traditional economic sense, you can compare the price of a good or service to a price index, such as the Consumer Price Index (CPI).

One way to think about purchasing power is to imagine that your salary is the same as your grandfather's salary 40 years ago. Today, you need a higher salary to maintain the same quality of life.

For the same reason, homebuyers looking for a home in the $300,000 to $350,000 price range 10 years ago had more and better options than people in the same price range today.

Purchasing power affects every aspect of an economy, from consumers buying goods to investors buying shares to a country's economic prosperity.

When the purchasing power of a currency is reduced due to excessive inflation, it can have severe negative economic consequences. These may include a higher cost of living, higher interest rates impacting global markets, and a downgraded credit rating. All these factors can lead to an economic crisis.

Purchasing power and CPI

Governments create policies and regulations to protect the purchasing power of currencies and keep the economy healthy. They also monitor economic data to keep abreast of changing conditions. For example, the US Bureau of Labour Statistics (BLS) measures price changes and publishes these changes through the CPI.

The CPI is one of the indicators for measuring inflation and purchasing power. It calculates the change in the weighted average prices of consumer goods and services, especially transport, food and healthcare, at a given point in time. The CPI can indicate both a change in the cost of living and deflation.

The CPI is just an official measure of US purchasing power.

Purchase price parity

The concept associated with purchasing power is called purchasing price party (PPP). Purchasing power parity is an economic theory that estimates the amount by which an item must be adjusted to parity given the exchange rates of two countries. Purchasing power parity can be used to compare economic activity, income levels, and other relevant data about the cost of living or likely levels of inflation and deflation across countries.

The World Bank's International Comparison Project publishes purchasing power parity data by country.

Loss or increase in purchasing power

Gain or loss in purchasing power is the decrease or increase in the amount of goods that a consumer can buy for a certain amount. When prices rise, consumers lose purchasing power. When prices fall, they gain purchasing power.

The reasons for the decline in purchasing power can be government regulation, inflation, natural and man-made disasters. Reasons for rising purchasing power include deflation and technological innovation.

An example of increased purchasing power is when a laptop that was selling for $1,000 two years ago is now selling for $500. Without inflation, $1,000 could buy a laptop plus $500 worth of goods.

purchasing power example

Germany after World War I

Historical examples of hyperinflation and hyperinflation (which can destroy the purchasing power of a currency) can show us the various causes and effects of this phenomenon. Sometimes costly and destructive wars lead to economic collapse, especially for failed states. This happened in Germany after the First World War (WWI).

After World War I in the 1920s, Germany faced extreme economic hardship and near-unprecedented hyperinflation, in part because Germany had to pay massive reparations.

Unable to pay these reparations in dubious Deutsche Marks, Germany printed paper money to buy foreign currency, leading to a high rate of inflation that rendered the Deutsche Mark worthless and unavailable for purchase.

2008 financial crisis

The impact of declining purchasing power after the 2008 global financial crisis and the sovereign debt crisis in Europe is remembered today. Thanks to increased globalization and the introduction of the euro, currencies are inextricably linked, and economic problems can cross geographical boundaries. As a result, governments around the world have developed policies to control inflation, protect purchasing power, and prevent recessions.

For example, in 2008 the Federal Reserve kept interest rates near zero and introduced a quantitative easing (QE) program. The initially controversial policy of quantitative easing was for the Federal Reserve (Fed) to buy government and other marketable securities in order to increase the money supply and lower interest rates.

The increase in capital stimulated an increase in lending and created more liquidity. As soon as the economy stabilized, the US stopped quantitative easing.

The European Central Bank (ECB) also carried out quantitative easing after the sovereign debt crisis in Europe to help stop deflation in the euro area and boost the purchasing power of the euro.

The European Economic and Monetary Union has set strict rules in the euro area regarding accurate reporting of sovereign debt, inflation and other financial data. As a rule, countries try to fix inflation at the level of 2%. Moderate inflation is acceptable. A high level of deflation can lead to economic stagnation.

Special attention items

Investments that protect against purchasing power risk

Retirees may be particularly aware of the loss of purchasing power, as many of them live on fixed amounts of money. They must ensure that their investments generate returns at or above the rate of inflation so that the value of their reserves does not decrease each year.

Bonds and fixed income investments are most exposed to purchasing power or inflation risk. Fixed annuities, certificates of deposit (CD) and treasury bills fall into this category. For example, long-term, lower fixed-income bonds may not increase your investment during times of inflation.

Certain investments or investment strategies can help protect investors from purchasing power risk. For example, US Treasury Inflation Protected Securities (TIPS) are adjusting to keep up with rising prices. Commodities such as oil and metals are more likely to retain their price power during periods of inflation.

What is purchasing power?

Purchasing power is how much you can buy with your money. When prices rise, your money can buy less. When prices drop, your money can buy more.

How does inflation reduce purchasing power?

Inflation is a gradual increase in prices for a wide range of goods and services. If inflation stays high or gets out of hand, it drains your purchasing power—what you can buy with your money. Due to inflation, the same item that was selling for $2 six months ago can now cost $4. This price increase, in turn, eats away at people's savings, which in turn undermines their standard of living.

What is the consumer price index?

The CPI measures the prices of certain consumer goods and services over time to identify price changes that indicate inflation. Prices for these goods and services are obtained from US consumers in the US Census Bureau of Labor Statistics Consumer Expenditure Survey (which publishes the CPI).

Bottom line

Long-term investors know that a loss of purchasing power can greatly affect their investment. Rising inflation affects purchasing power by reducing the amount of goods or services you can buy with your money.

CHAPTER FOURTEEN

WEIGHTED AVERAGE

A weighted average is a calculation that takes into account the varying degrees of importance of numbers in a data set. When calculating the weighted average, each number in the data set is multiplied by a predetermined weight before the final calculation is performed.

- A weighted average is more accurate than a simple average when all numbers in the dataset are given the same weight.
- The weighted average takes into account the relative importance or frequency of certain factors in the data set.
- A weighted average is sometimes more accurate than a simple average.
- With a weighted average, each data point value is multiplied by the assigned weight, which is then summed and divided by the number of data points.

Therefore, weighted averaging can improve the accuracy of the data.

Equity investors use weighted averages to track the value of stocks purchased over time.

What is the purpose of the weighted average?

When calculating a prime or arithmetic mean, all numbers are treated the same and have equal weight. But the weights assigned by the weighted average can determine the relative importance of each data point.

A weighted average is usually calculated to equalize the frequency of values in a data set. For example, a survey may collect enough responses from each age group to be considered statistically significant, but relative to their proportion in the population, there may be more respondents in the 18–34 age group than in all other age groups with fewer respondents. The survey team may weigh the results for the 18-34 age group so that their views are reflected appropriately.

However, the values in the data set may be weighted for reasons other than frequency of occurrence. For example, if students in a dance class are assessed based on skills, attendance, and demeanour, skill assessment may be more important than other factors.

In either case, the weighted average multiplies each data point value by the assigned weight, which is then summed and divided by the number of data points.

In a weighted average, the final average reflects the relative importance of each observation and is therefore more informative than a simple average. It also results in smoother data and improved accuracy.

Weighted average

Data point	Data point value	Assign weight	Data point weight value
1	10	2	20
1	50	5	250
1	40	3	120
Total	100	10	390
Weighted average			39

Weighted Equity Portfolio

Investors typically form stock positions over several years. This makes it difficult to track the relative changes in the cost base of these reserves and their value.

Investors can calculate the weighted average price of shares paid for shares. To do this, multiply the number of shares purchased at each price by that price, add up the values, and divide the total value by the total number of shares.

For example,

suppose an investor buys 100 shares of a company for $10 in the first year and 50 shares of the same stock for $40 in the second year. To obtain a weighted average of the price paid, investors multiply 100 shares by $10 in the first year, 50 shares by $40 in the second year, and add the results for a total of $3,000. Then divide the total amount paid for the shares ($3,000 in this case) by the number of shares purchased in two years, 150, to get the weighted average price paid of $20.

This average is now weighted by the number of shares purchased at each price, not just the absolute price.

Weighted Average Example

In addition to stock purchase prices, weighted averages appear in many areas of finance, including portfolio returns, inventory accounting, and valuation.

When a fund holding multiple securities makes a 10% return in a year, that 10% is the fund's weighted average return relative to the value of each position in the fund.

For example,

for inventory accounting, the weighted average of inventory takes into account fluctuations in commodity prices, while LIFO (last in, first out) or FIFO (first in, first out) methods focus more on time than cost.

Investors use the weighted average cost of capital (WACC) to discount a company's cash flows when valuing a company to determine if its shares are valued correctly. WACC is weighted according to the market value of debt and equity in the company's capital structure.

How is a weighted average different from a simple average?

The weighted average takes into account the relative contribution or weight of the things being averaged, whereas the simple average does not. Therefore, it assigns more value to those elements that appear relatively larger on average.

What are examples of weighted averages used in finance?

Many weighted averages can be found in finance, including the weighted average price by volume (VWAP), the weighted average cost of capital (WACC), and the exponential moving average (EMA) used in charts. Portfolio weights and the LIFO and FIFO inventory methods also use weighted averages.

How is the weighted average calculated?

You can calculate a weighted average by successively multiplying its relative shares or percentages by its values and adding these sums. So, if the portfolio is 55% stocks, 40% bonds, and 5% cash, these weights will be multiplied by their annual returns to get the weighted average returns. So if stocks, bonds, and cash return 10%, 5%, and 2%, respectively, the weighted average return would be

$(0.55 \times 10\%) + (0.40 \times 5\%) + (0.05 \times 2\%) = 7.6\%$.

COST OF LIVING

The cost of living is a measure of the cost of living in a specific location at a specific time based on factors such as rent, gas, and food costs.

The cost of living refers to the amount of income required to maintain a certain lifestyle in a certain place at a certain point in time. The cost of living varies geographically and over time, meaning that the cost of the same lifestyle often varies from region to region, and in any particular region, the cost may rise (or, in rare cases, fall) over time.

The cost of living is the amount needed to pay for basic expenses such as housing, food, taxes, and healthcare in a specific location and time period. The cost of living is often used to compare the cost of living in one city to another. The cost of living is tied to wages. For example, if spending is higher in a city like New York, wages must be higher so that people can afford to live in that city.

Cost of living and lifestyle

The cost of living can be an important factor in a person's wealth accumulation, as wages can provide a higher standard of living in a city with less daily expenses such as rent, food, and entertainment. On the contrary, in expensive cities like New York, high salaries may seem insufficient. A 2018 survey by global staffing firm Mercer found that the cities with the highest cost of living included Hong Kong, the Angolan capital Luanda, Tokyo, Zurich and Singapore, in that order. New York was named the most expensive city in the US, followed by San Francisco and Los Angeles, Chicago, Washington DC and Boston.

For example,

If we assume that a person can lead a simple but comfortable lifestyle, including a modest apartment, medical care, food, public transportation, and enough extra money to save money and go out a few times a month, then the annual income in city A will be $39,000. , a medium-sized suburb. The same lifestyle might require a $49,000 annual income in City B, a more populous metropolitan area where rent, food, and other expenses are higher. In this case, the cost of living in city B is significantly higher than in city A.

Another way to think about the cost of living is to compare what you can get for a certain salary in one place and another. For example, with an annual income of $85,000 in Fort Wayne, Indiana, the average citizen can have enough left after taking care of things like housing, food, and taxes. On the other hand, in Manhattan, New York, the same income is barely enough for the bare necessities, leaving little for casual purchases. This is because goods and services, including essentials such as rent and food, cost much more on average in Manhattan than in Fort Wayne.

Because the cost of living varies across the US, wages are higher where costs such as rent, food, and gas are higher. For this reason, the same jobs can be paid differently in different places.

Cost of living index

The Cost of Living Index compares the cost of living in major cities to their respective metropolitan areas. The index includes the cost of various living expenses, creating a general measure that beginners can use as a benchmark. The index provides informative information on rent, transportation and grocery spending as college graduates weigh employment options and those who are currently looking for work consider moving.

Different indicators can calculate the cost of living differently. For example, in 2018, Kiplinger found that the most expensive city according to the Council for Public and Economic Research was San Diego, not New York. The Council's Cost of Living Index measures the cost of things like housing, groceries, utilities, transportation and healthcare, and even a haircut or a movie, in 269 metropolitan areas. In San Diego, for example, housing costs are 138% higher than the national average, and transportation costs are more than 20% higher than the national average.

Cost of living and salary

The rise in the cost of living has sparked controversy about the U.S. federal minimum wage and the gap between the legally allowed minimum wage and the income needed to maintain an adequate cost of living. Proponents of wage increases point out that productivity increases since 1968 have been unfairly tied to the minimum wage. Because wage levels once tracked productivity growth, the gap between earnings and labour productivity has reached historically disproportionate levels. In contrast, opponents of the minimum wage argue that higher minimum wages can drive consumer prices up as employers offset rising labour costs.

Wage Growth and Cost of Living Adjustment (COLA)

In 1973, Congress passed the Cost of Living Adjustment Act (COLA). COLA adjusts Social Security and Supplemental Security Income (SSI) benefits to keep payments in line with inflation. For example, in December 2018, COLA was 2.8%, and the increased amount will be paid from January 2019. The levels of federal SSI payments increased by the same percentage.

The Social Security Act requires COLA to be based on an increase in the Consumer Price Index (CPI-W) for city employees and employees. The Social Security Administration stated:

The COLA effective as of December of the current year is equal to the percentage increase (if any) of the CPI-W from the average in the third quarter of the current year to the average in the third quarter of the previous year, where COLA becomes as a result.

The cost of living is the amount needed to maintain a certain standard of living by paying for things like housing, food, taxes, and health care.

Wages should reflect the higher cost of living in more expensive cities like New York.

The Cost of Living Index compares the cost of living in major cities to their respective metropolitan areas.

PRODUCER PRICE INDEX (PPI)

PPI is a measure of the weighted average price of all Phase 1 commodities produced in the United States, such as metals, lumber, and natural gas.

The Producer Price Index (PPI) is a monthly estimate of the weighted average price that an American "manufacturer" (e.g. suppliers, wholesalers, etc.) earns for goods and services (mainly for other businesses) created for him. In other words, it is an estimate of the average value of all Phase 1 domestic goods and services in a given month.

The producer price index, like the consumer price index (CPI), is an important economic indicator calculated and released monthly by the US Bureau of Labour Statistics.

The Producer Price Index (PPI) measures the average change over time in the prices of products received by domestic producers. It is a measure of inflation at the wholesale level, compiled from thousands of indices that measure producer prices by industry and product category. The index is published monthly by the US Bureau of Labour Statistics (BLS). The PPI is different from the consumer price index (CPI), which measures changes in the prices consumers pay for goods and services.

The Producer Price Index measures changes in prices paid to US producers of goods and services.

The PPI is a measure of wholesale inflation, while the consumer price index measures the prices consumers pay.

The index is published monthly by the Bureau of Labour Statistics.

The PPI index is calculated based on products and services, industries and buyers' economic identity and is used to calculate the total monthly PPI change in final demand.

The index calculates price changes for private contracts based on supplier entry prices.

Understanding Producer Price Index (PPI)

PPI measures inflation (or, more rarely, deflation) from the perspective of a product manufacturer or service provider. Producer and consumer price trends are unlikely to diverge in the long run, as producer prices can strongly influence prices charged to consumers, and vice versa. In the short term, wholesale and retail inflation may differ due to distribution costs, government taxes and subsidies.

The BLS releases the PPI and its constituent industry and commodity indices in the second week of the month following the survey key date. It is based on approximately 100,000 monthly quotations published voluntarily on the

Internet by more than 25,000 manufacturers, which are systematically selected. The survey covers all US output of goods and approximately 71% of service costs. The index of products and services that composes it is weighted based on the value of output in that category to calculate the overall change in producer prices.

PPI is used to forecast inflation and calculate escalator clauses in private contracts based on the prices of basic inputs. It is also important for tracking price changes across industries and comparing wholesale and retail price trends.

Producer price index (PPI) and consumer price index (CPI)

Both PPI and CPI are important economic indicators as they indicate monthly price changes. But they reflect prices from different angles.

As mentioned above, the Producer Price Index measures prices based on the first commercial transaction of a product or service. It measures the value of goods and services when they first leave their place of origin – when they are wholesaled by producers (often to other businesses, often going through many stages before reaching the consumer). Sales tax is not included in the PPI ingredient price, and imports are not included because the PPI only counts domestic products.

This is different from the consumer price index (CPI), which measures price changes that consumers experience.

The Consumer Price Index (CPI) measures the average cost of goods and services purchased by US consumers (i.e. end users). In other words, it is a calculation of the estimated value of goods and services at their final destination (citizens), so it includes imported goods and services, and sales tax is included in the price of its constituents.

The focus of CPI is on end sales. But these two indices differ not only in the type of price being measured. There are also important compositional differences between PPI and CPI that can be taken into account. These differences are based on each inclusion and omission.

For example, the PPI does not measure price changes in total housing costs, while the CPI housing category (including implied landlord-equivalent rent) is one-third of the overall index. Meanwhile, PPI contains nearly 18 percent of health care products and services, not far from the industry's nearly 20 percent weight in US gross domestic product (GDP). In contrast, the weight of the CPI on health is less than 9%. This is because it does not measure third party health care reimbursement. Another key difference is that, unlike the CPI, the PPI does not include the price of imported goods. Conversely, PPI includes export prices, while CPI does not.

(REITS) REAL ESTATE INVESTMENT TRUSTS

What is a REIT?

REITs or Real Estate Investment Trusts can be described as companies that own and manage real estate to generate income. REIT is a company that manages a portfolio of high-value real estate and mortgages.

For example,

They rent out real estate and collect rent from it. The rent thus collected is then distributed to shareholders in the form of income and dividends.

Typically, REITs provide investors with the opportunity to own expensive real estate and allow them to earn dividend income to ultimately raise capital. Thus, investors can take advantage of the opportunity to evaluate their capital and earn income at the same time.

Investors big and small can put their money into this investment option and reap the rewards accordingly. Small investors may try to pool their resources with other investors and invest in large commercial real estate projects. Assets in REITs include data centers, infrastructure, medical facilities, residential complexes, and more.

How REITs work

Congress established the REIT in 1960 as an amendment to expand the excise tax on cigars. The provision allows investors to buy shares in commercial real estate portfolios - previously only the wealthy could access them through large financial intermediaries.

Real estate in a REIT portfolio may include residential complexes, data centers, medical facilities, hotels, infrastructure (in the form of fiber optic cables, cell towers and power pipes), office buildings, shopping malls, warehouses, woodlands, and warehouses.

Generally, REITs are focused on a specific real estate sector. However, a diversified and specialized REIT may have different types of real estate in its portfolio, for example, a REIT consisting of office and retail real estate. Many REITs are publicly traded on the major stock exchanges and investors can buy and sell them like stocks during the trading session. These REITs are usually heavily traded and are considered highly liquid instruments.

How does a company qualify as a REIT?

To qualify as a REIT, a company must meet certain requirements, as described below.

The organization must be structured as a business trust or company.

Extended fully transferable shares.

Managed by a team of trustees or a board of directors.

There must be at least 100 shareholders.

In each tax year, less than 5 individuals must not own 50% of their shares.

Requires payment of at least 90% of taxable income in the form of dividends.

Earn at least 75% of your gross income from mortgage interest or rent.

Up to 20% of the company's assets include shares in taxable REIT subsidiaries.

At least 75% of investment assets must be real estate.

At least 95% of the REIT's gross income must be invested.

Types of Real Estate Investment Trusts (REITs)

More broadly, the types of commercial REITs involved tend to help classify them better. In addition, methods aimed at selling and buying shares also help in the classification of REITs.

Below is a list of different types of REITs.

Equity: This type of REIT is the most popular. As a rule, this is associated with the operation and management of income-generating commercial real estate. It is noteworthy that rent is a frequent source of income here.

Mortgage: Also known as mREIT, it primarily includes homeowner lending and mortgage expansion. In addition, REITs typically purchase mortgage-backed securities. Mortgage REITs also generate income in the form of accrued interest on the money provided to the owners.

Hybrid: This option allows investors to diversify their portfolio by investing in mortgage and equity REITs. Therefore, both rent and interest are sources of income for this particular type of REIT.

Private REITs: These trusts function like private placements, serving only certain investors. As a rule, private REITs are not traded on national stock exchanges and are not registered with SEBI.

Publicly traded REITs: As a rule, publicly traded REITs are expanded with shares listed on national stock exchanges and regulated by SEBI. Individual investors can buy and sell such shares through the NSE.

Public non-trading REITs: These are unregistered REITs registered with SEBI. However, they are not traded on national stock exchanges. In addition, these options are less liquid when competing with public non-tradable REITs. In addition, they are more stable because they are not affected by market fluctuations.

REIT Benefits or Advantages of REITs

Investors who keep their money in REITs can enjoy the following benefits.

- Stable Dividend Income and Capital Gains: Investments in REITs are believed to provide significant dividend income as well as provide long-term stable capital gains.
- Diversification Options: Because most REITs are frequently traded on stock exchanges, this gives investors the opportunity to diversify their holdings.
- Transaction Transparency: REITs regulated by SEBI are required to provide professionally audited financial statements. It provides investors with the opportunity to use information about taxation, ownership and zoning, making the whole process transparent.
- Liquidity: Most REITs are traded on public stock exchanges, making them easier to buy and sell, which increases their liquidity.
- Total risk-adjusted return: Investing in REITs provides people with risk-adjusted returns and helps generate stable cash flow. This allows them to have a stable source of income even when inflation is high.
-

REIT restrictions

No tax credits: REITs don't help much when it comes to tax savings. For example, dividends received from REITs are taxable.

Market risks: One of the main risks associated with a REIT is its susceptibility to market fluctuations. This is why investors with weaker risk appetite should weigh up the return on these investments in advance.

Low growth prospects: REITs have fairly low capital appreciation prospects. This is mainly because they return up to 90% of their profits to investors and the remaining 10% is reinvested in their business.

The attached table shows the pros and cons of investing in the best REITs.

Pros	Cons
Liquidity	Lack of tax benefits
Option to diversify	Market risk
Transparent	Low growth prospect
Risk-adjusted returns	High maintenance fee
Steady dividend income	Other additional charges

Who should invest in REITs?

Because REITs own and manage high-value real estate, they are one of the most expensive ways to invest. So, investors who keep their money in REITs are those who have a lot of money at their disposal. For example, large institutional investors such as insurance companies, endowments, trust divisions of banks, pension funds, etc. may appropriately invest in these financial instruments.

The Role of REITs in Retirement Portfolios

Including REITs in a retirement portfolio is generally a good investment for a number of reasons. The following tips can help you gain valuable information.

Leverage your investment portfolio to a diversified real estate portfolio

By including real estate, you can diversify your asset class significantly without having to personally manage them. In addition, with diversification, price fluctuations in other investment options do not affect REITs. Conversely, it can be argued that REITs do not fall in value as quickly as stocks in a falling market.

Income opportunity

When the value of a REIT rises, investors tend to be rewarded handsomely. In addition, these companies must distribute 90% of their taxable income to their shareholders in order to generate a stable income.

Suitable for long term

Unlike stocks and bonds, which follow a 6-year business cycle, REITs are more in line with the real estate market. It is worth noting that such moves typically last over ten years, making them more suitable for investors looking for long-term investments. In turn, this has proven to be a profitable investment direction for retirement planning.

Helps to hedge against inflation

According to research, REITs allow investors to hedge against inflation in the long run. For example, with a 5-year investment horizon, investors can protect their money from inflation more effectively than with stock options.

How to invest in REITs?

As with popular public stocks, investors may choose to buy shares in a particular REIT listed on a major stock exchange. They can do this in three ways.

Stock: Individuals who are looking for a more direct way to invest in REITs should consider investing in stocks.

Mutual Funds: By choosing this option, individuals will be able to significantly diversify their portfolios. Because it is an indirect investment method, investors need to invest in such funds through a mutual fund company.

Exchange Traded Funds: With this special investment option, investors can indirectly own real estate and benefit from its diversification.

It is worth noting that REITs as an investment option are generally similar to mutual funds, with the only difference being that REITs own real estate rather than bonds or stock options. In addition, REIT investors have the right to seek the help of a financial advisor to make a more informed decision about investing in their respective REIT options.

REIT Valuation Tips

If investors take into account the tips below, they will be able to effectively assess the value of a particular REIT.

Before investing in any particular REIT, investors should look for companies with a proven track record of delivering high dividend yields. In addition, they analysed the company's role in promoting long-term capital gains.

Investors can diversify their portfolios by buying shares through the stock exchange without having to invest in the long term.

Investors should invest their money in REITs that have different properties and tenants.

They should choose ETFs and mutual funds that invest in REITs. Since these funds come from professional assistance, investors will be able to manage them more skillfully.

It will be more beneficial to choose a company that has been in the field for several years and has an experienced core team.

Finally, individuals must clearly state how their investment will be compensated. For example, they should analyse the REIT's management team and its performance indicators using measures such as funds from operations or financial management ratios. Similarly, it will be helpful to consider REIT earnings-per-share growth and current dividend income before investing in order to maximise returns.

CHAPTER FIFTEEN

UNEMPLOYMENT

The term unemployment refers to a situation in which a person is actively seeking work but is unable to find one. Unemployment is considered a key indicator of the health of an economy.

The most commonly used measure of unemployment is the unemployment rate. It is calculated by dividing the number of unemployed people by the number of people in the labor force.

Many governments offer unemployment insurance for certain unemployed people who meet eligibility criteria.

- Unemployment occurs when workers who want to work cannot find work.
- A high unemployment rate predicts an economic crisis, and an extremely low unemployment rate can signal overheating.
- Unemployment can be classified as frictional, cyclical, structural or institutional.
- Government agencies collect and publish unemployment data in a variety of ways.
- Many governments provide the unemployed with a small income through unemployment insurance if they meet certain requirements.

Understanding Unemployment

Unemployment is a key economic indicator because it measures the ability (or inability) of workers to get paid work and contribute to the production of the economy. More unemployed means less overall economic output.

The definition of unemployment does not include people who leave the labor market for reasons such as retirement, higher education, or disability.

Sign of Economic Distress

The unemployed must at least maintain a living wage during the period of unemployment. This means that countries with high unemployment have lower output without a proportional fall in demand for basic consumption.

Continued high unemployment could portend serious economic problems and even lead to social and political unrest.

Signs of overheating

On the other hand, low unemployment means the economy is likely to operate near full capacity, maximising output, stimulating wage growth, and raising living standards over time.

However, the extremely low unemployment rate could also be a warning sign of an overheated economy, inflationary pressures and austerity conditions facing businesses needing additional workers.

Unemployment category

While the definition of unemployment is clear, economists divide unemployment into many different categories. The two broadest categories are voluntary unemployment and involuntary unemployment. When unemployment is voluntary, it means that a person voluntarily leaves work in search of another job. When it is involuntary, it means that the person was fired or fired, and now he must look for another job.

Type of unemployment

Unemployment – both voluntary and involuntary – can be divided into four types.

Frictional unemployment

Such unemployment is usually short-lived. It is also the least problematic from an economic point of view. This happens when people change jobs voluntarily. After a person leaves the company, it is natural to look for another job. Similarly, graduates who are just starting to look for work to enter the labour force increase frictional unemployment.

Frictional unemployment is a natural consequence of the fact that market processes take time and information costs are high. Finding new jobs, recruiting new employees, and matching the right people to the right jobs all take time and effort. This leads to frictional unemployment.

Cyclical unemployment

Cyclical unemployment is the change in the number of unemployed during economic ups and downs, such as those associated with changes in oil prices. Unemployment rises during a recession and falls during economic growth.

Preventing and mitigating cyclical unemployment during recessions is one of the main reasons to study economics and the various policy instruments that governments use to stimulate the economy during business cycle downturns.

structural unemployment

Structural unemployment occurs as a result of technological changes in the economic structure in which the labour market operates. Technological change can lead to unemployment of workers fired from jobs no longer needed. Examples of such changes include the replacement of horse-drawn carriages by cars and the automation of manufacturing,

Retraining these workers can be difficult, costly, and time-consuming. Displaced workers often end up either permanently unemployed or dropping out of the labor force altogether.

Institutional unemployment

Institutional unemployment is the result of long-term or permanent institutional factors and incentives in the economy. The following situations can cause an organization to lose a job:

How to measure unemployment

In the US, the government uses surveys, censuses, and unemployment insurance claims to track unemployment.

The US Census Bureau conducts a monthly survey called the Current Population Survey (CPS) on behalf of the US Bureau of Labour Statistics (BLS) to provide a preliminary estimate of the country's unemployment rate. The survey has been conducted monthly since 1940. The sample includes about 60,000 eligible households. This means about 110,000 people per month. The census changes a quarter of the sampled households every month, so no household is represented for more than four consecutive months. This is necessary to improve the reliability of estimates.

There are many variants of the unemployment rate, with different definitions of who is unemployed and who is in the labour force.

The BLS generally uses the U-3 unemployment rate (defined as the total number of unemployed as a percentage of the civilian labour force) as the official unemployment rate. However, this definition does not include the desperate unemployed who are no longer looking for work.

Other categories of the unemployed include desperate workers and part-time or part-time workers who want to work full-time but are unable to do so for financial reasons.

History of unemployment

Although the US government began tracking unemployment in the 1940s, the highest unemployment rate to date was during the Great Depression, when the unemployment rate rose to 24.9% in 1933.

Unemployment remained above 14% between 1931 and 1940, but then fell to single digits. It remained there until it exceeded 10% in 1982. In 2009, during the Great Recession, unemployment rose again to 10%. In April 2020, during the coronavirus pandemic, the unemployment rate reached 14.8%. The ratio has been declining since June 2021.

As of May 2022, the unemployment rate stood at 3.6%, unchanged from the previous month.

What is the main reason for unemployment?

There are many reasons for unemployment. These include recessions, depressions, technological improvements, job outsourcing, and voluntarily leaving one job in search of another.

What are the three types of unemployment?

Today, economists distinguish three main types of unemployment: frictional, structural and cyclical. Frictional unemployment is the result of a change in voluntary employment in the economy. Frictional unemployment occurs naturally even in a growing, stable economy when workers change jobs. Structural unemployment can be permanently devastating due to the fundamental and permanent changes taking place in the structure of the economy. These changes may lead to the marginalization of a group of workers. These include technological change, lack of appropriate skills, and job transfers to another country abroad. Cyclical unemployment is related to the loss of jobs that occurs during changes in the business cycle.

What is the strict definition of unemployment?

The official definition of unemployment comes from the US Bureau of Labor Statistics, which states that "People are classified as unemployed if they are unemployed, have been actively seeking work in the last 4 weeks, and are currently available to work."

CHAPTER SIXTEEN

BUSINESS CYCLE

A business cycle is a fluctuation in a country's overall economic activity—a cycle consisting of an almost simultaneous expansion of many economic activities followed by a similar general decline (downturn). This series of changes is repeated, but not cyclical.

- The business cycle consists of coordinated cyclical ups and downs in broad measures of economic activity—output, employment, income, and sales.
- The alternating phases of the business cycle are expansions and contractions (also known as recessions).
- Recessions usually begin at the peak of the business cycle—when the upturn ends—and end at the bottom of the business cycle, when the next upturn begins.
- The severity of a recession is measured by the three D's: depth, spread, and duration, while the strength of a rise is measured by how obvious, widespread, and sustained it is.

Understanding the business cycle

In essence, the business cycle is characterized by the alternation of phases of expansion and contraction of aggregate economic activity, as well as the relationship between economic variables in each phase of the cycle. Aggregate economic activity is represented not only by real (i.e., inflation-adjusted) GDP, a measure of total output, but also by aggregates of industrial production, employment, income, and sales, which are used to measure key timed economic indicators. for the economy. The official definition of the peaks and lows of the US economic cycle.

A popular misconception is that a recession is simply defined as two consecutive quarters of decline in real GDP. Notably, the 1960–1961 and 2001 recessions did not include two consecutive quarters of real GDP decline.

A recession is actually a special kind of vicious circle, where a cascade of declines in production, employment, income, and sales in turn leads to a further decline in production, spreading rapidly from one industry to another and from one region to another...

This domino effect is the key to spreading the weakness of the recession throughout the economy, resulting in a link between these simultaneous economic performances and the continuation of the recession.

Economic downturn

On the other hand, when the vicious cycle of recession reverses and becomes virtuous, the business cycle begins to recover, with an increase in output leading to more employment, higher incomes and higher sales, which leads to further growth in output. The recovery can only continue and lead to sustained economic growth if it is self-sustaining—a domino effect that spreads the recovery across the economy.

Restore

Of course, the stock market is not the economy. Therefore, the business cycle should not be confused with the market cycle as measured by a broad stock price index.

Measuring and dating the business cycle

The severity of a recession is measured by three D factors: depth, spread, and duration. The depth of the recession depends on the sharp decline in broad indicators of production, employment, income, and sales. Its spread is measured by the extent to which it spreads across economic activities, industries and geographic areas. Its duration is determined by the time interval between peaks and troughs.

In the same way, the strength of an expansion depends on its evidence, prevalence, and permanence. The three P's correspond to the three D's of decay.

The expansion starts at the bottom (or bottom) of the business cycle and continues to the next peak, and the decline begins at that peak and continues to the next low.

The National Bureau of Economic Research (NBER) determines the chronology of the business cycle – the dates of the beginning and end of recessions and booms in the US economy. Thus, his Business Cycle Dating Committee considers a recession to be "a marked decline in economic activity in an economy lasting more than a few months and usually manifesting itself in real GDP, real income, employment, industrial production, wholesale and retail trade." sales."

Dating committees often set recession start and end dates well in advance of recession. For example, after the end of the 2007–2009 recession, he "waited until July 30, 2010 and August 27, 2010 to announce revisions to the national income and product accounts" and announced the June 2009 recession's end date of September 20, 2010. Since the committee's inception in 1979, the average delay between the announcement of recession start and end dates has been 8 months at its peak and 15 months at its trough.

Before the committee was formed, from 1949 to 1978, recession start and end dates were determined by Dr. Jeffrey H. Moore on behalf of the NBER. He then served as a senior member of the committee from 1979 until his death in 2000. In 1996, Moore co-founded the Economic Cycle Research Institute (ECRI), which determines business cycle chronologies for 21 other economies, including the G7 and Gold, based on the same methodology used to determine the official U.S. business cycle chronology. country. In analyses that need to be compared with international recession dates, the most widely used procedure is to refer to NBER dates in the US and ECRI dates in other countries.

A US economic recovery usually lasts longer than a US recession. From 1854 to 1899 they were almost the same in duration, with recessions averaging 24 months and booms 27 months. Then the average length of a recession was reduced to 18 months between 1900 and 1945 and to 11 months after World War II. At the same time, the average duration of expansion gradually increased: from 27 months in 1854-1899. up to 32 months in 1900-1945, up to 45 months in 1945-1982, up to 103 months in 1982-2009.

The depth of the recession has varied over time. They, as a rule, go very deep into the pre-war (WWII) period, going back to the 19th century. With the sharp decline in cyclicality after World War II, the depth of the recession was significantly reduced. From the mid-1980s until the eve of the Great Recession of 2007-2009—a period sometimes referred to as the Great Moderation—cyclical volatility further declined. What's more, the expansion's average lifespan has roughly doubled since the start of the Great Moderation.

Variety of cycling experiences

The experience of most market economies before World War II included deep recessions and strong booms. However, the post-World War II recovery in many major economies, after the devastation that the war had inflicted on many major economies, resulted in a strong upward trend that lasted for decades.

With strong trending growth, as China has demonstrated in recent decades, cyclical downturns are difficult to keep growth below zero and lead to a recession. For the same reason, Germany and Italy did not experience their first recession after World War II until the mid-1960s and thus experienced two decades of growth. From the 1950s to the 1970s, France experienced a 15-year expansion, Britain experienced a 22-year expansion, and Japan experienced a 19-year expansion. From the late 1950s to the early 1980s, Canada experienced 23 years of growth. Even the United States experienced the longest period of expansion in its history, spanning almost nine years from the beginning of 1961 to the end of 1969.

Since business cycle recessions are much rarer, economists have focused on growth cycles, which include alternating periods of growth above and below the trend. But monitoring growth cycles requires identifying current trends, which is problematic for predicting business cycles in real time. Geoffrey H. Moore of ECRI proposed a different cycle concept, the growth rate cycle.

Growth cycles, also known as acceleration-deceleration cycles, consist of alternating periods of cyclical ups and downs in economic growth, measured by the growth rates of the same key simultaneous economic indicators that are used to determine the peaks and troughs of the business cycle. In this sense, the growth rate cycle (GRC) is the first derivative of the classical business cycle (BC). Importantly, however, GRC analysis does not require trend evaluation.

Using a methodology similar to that used to determine the business cycle timeline, ECRI has also determined the GRC timeline for 22 countries, including the US.

Since GRCs are based on business cycle inflection points, they are especially useful for investors who are sensitive to the links between the stock market and the business cycle.

CHAPTER SEVENTEEN

BEHAVIOURAL ECONOMICS

What is behavioural economics?

Behavioral economics is the study of psychology related to the economic decision-making process of individuals and institutions. The two most important questions in this area are:

- Are economists' assumptions about utility or profit maximization a good approximation to the actual behavior of people?
- Does the individual maximize subjective expected utility?

Behavioral economics is often associated with normative economics.

Learn about behavioral economics

In an ideal world, people would always make the best decisions that would bring them the most benefit and satisfaction. In economics, rational choice theory states that when people are faced with multiple options in the face of scarcity, they choose the option that maximizes personal satisfaction. The theory suggests that people, given their preferences and limitations, are capable of making rational decisions, effectively weighing the costs and benefits of each option available to them. The final decision will be the person's best choice. Rational people have self-control, are not influenced by emotions and external factors, and therefore know what is best for them. Alas, behavioural economics explains that people are irrational and incapable of making good decisions.

Behavioural economics uses psychology and economics to study why people sometimes make irrational decisions and why and how their behaviour does not match the predictions of economic models. Decisions such as how much to spend on a cup of coffee, whether to go to graduate school. Whether to lead a healthy lifestyle, and how much to save for retirement, are decisions that most people make at some point in their lives. Life. Behavioural economics tries to explain why people prefer A over B.

Because people are emotional and easily distracted, they make decisions that are not in their best interests. For example, according to rational choice theory, if Charles wants to lose weight, and he has information about the number of calories in each edible product, he will choose only the food with the fewest calories. Behavioral economics argues that even if Charles wanted to lose weight and chose to eat healthy, his behavior would eventually be affected by cognitive biases, emotions, and social influences. If a television ad advertises an attractively priced brand of ice cream and claims that each person needs 2,000 calories a day to function effectively, ice cream's desirable image, price, and seemingly effective characteristics may lull Charles into sweetness. The temptation to break away from the weight loss trend shows his lack of self-control.

Statement

One application of behavioural economics is heuristics, the use of rules of thumb or mental shortcuts to make quick decisions. However, heuristics can lead to cognitive biases when decisions are made that lead to errors. Behavioural game theory is a new category of game theory that can also be applied to behavioural economics because game theory conducts experiments and analyses the decisions that people make irrationally. Another area where behavioural economics can be applied is behavioural finance, which attempts to explain why investors make rash decisions when trading capital markets.

Companies are increasingly using behavioural economics to increase sales of their products. In 2007, an 8 GB iPhone cost $600, but that figure soon dropped to $400. What if the intrinsic value of the phone was $400? If Apple released the phone for $400, the initial smartphone market reaction to the price could be negative, as the phone might seem too expensive. But by releasing the phone at a higher price and dropping it to $400, consumers thought they were getting a good deal, and Apple's sales skyrocketed. Also, consider a soap manufacturer that makes the same soap but sells it in two different packages to appeal to multiple target groups. One package advertises the soap for all soap users, and the other for sensitive skin consumers. If the packaging does not indicate that the soap is for sensitive skin, then the latter will not buy the product. They choose a soap with a label for sensitive skin, even though it's the exact same product in a regular package.

As companies begin to understand that their consumers are irrational, an effective approach to incorporating behavioural economics into a company's decision-making policy, involving its internal and external stakeholders, can prove beneficial.

CHAPTER EIGHTEEN

RATIONAL CHOICE THEORY

What is rational choice theory?

A key premise of rational choice theory is that people do not choose goods that are in stock for a reason. Instead, they use a logical decision-making process that weighs different options based on their costs and benefits.

Who created rational choice theory?

Adam Smith, who developed the idea of the "invisible hand" governing the free market economy in the mid-1770s, is generally regarded as the father of rational choice theory. Smith discussed the theory of the invisible hand in his 1776 book An Inquiry into the Nature and Causes of the Wealth of Nations.

What is the main purpose of rational choice theory?

The main goal of rational choice theory is to explain why individuals and larger groups of people make certain choices given certain costs and rewards. According to rational choice theory, people make choices based on their own interests, which will bring them the greatest benefit. People weigh their options and do what they think is best for them.

What is rational choice theory in international relations?

Nations, IGOs, NGOs and transnational corporations are all made up of people. To understand the behavior of these entities, we must understand the behavior of the people who control them. Rational choice theory helps explain how leaders and other important decision makers in organizations and institutions make decisions. Rational choice theory can also try to predict the future actions of these actors.

What are the benefits of rational choice theory?

One of the strengths of rational choice theory is the versatility of its applications. It can be applied to many disciplines and fields of study. He also makes reasonable guesses and compelling logic. The theory also encourages people to make smart economic decisions. By making smart economic decisions, people can get more tools that will allow them to further increase their preferences in the future.

The bottom lines

Much of classical economic theory is based on the assumption of rational choice theory: people make the choice that brings them the greatest benefit or utility. In addition, people are more likely to prefer actions that will benefit them than actions that will be neutral or harm them. Despite many criticisms of rational choice theory (due to the fact that people are emotional and easily distracted, and their behavior does not always match the predictions of economic models). It is still widely used in various disciplines and fields of research.

What is rational choice theory?

Rational choice theory states that people use rational computation to make rational choices and achieve outcomes that are consistent with their personal goals. These results are also related to the maximization of self-interest. Given the limited options available to them, the use of rational choice theory is expected to lead to outcomes that bring people the most benefit and satisfaction.

Rational choice theory states that people rely on rational calculations to make rational choices that lead to outcomes that serve their interests.

Rational choice theory is often associated with concepts such as rational actors, self-interest, and the invisible hand.

Many economists believe that the factors associated with rational choice theory are good for the economy as a whole.

Adam Smith was one of the first economists to offer the basic principles of rational choice theory.

Many economists question the validity of rational choice theory and the invisible hand theory.

Understanding rational choice theory

Many mainstream economic assumptions and theories are based on rational choice theory. Rational choice theory is related to the concepts of rational actors, self-interest, and the invisible hand.

Rational choice theory is based on the assumption that rational actors are involved in the process. Rational actors are those in the economy who make rational choices based on calculations and the information available to them. Rational actors form the basis of rational choice theory. Rational choice theory suggests that individuals or rational actors in any situation actively try to maximise their benefits and therefore always try to minimise their losses.

Economists can use this rationality assumption as part of a broader study of understanding certain behaviours in society as a whole.

Self-Interest and the Invisible Hand

Adam Smith was one of the first economists to offer the basic principles of rational choice theory. Smith elaborated on his studies of self-interest and the theory of the invisible hand in his 1776 book An Inquiry into the Nature and Causes of the Wealth of Nations.

The invisible hand itself is a metaphor for the invisible forces that influence the free market economy. First, the invisible hand theory involves self-interest. Both this theory and further developments in rational choice theory refute any negative self-interest fallacies. Rather, these concepts suggest that rational actors acting in their own interests can actually create benefits for the economy as a whole.

According to the theory of the invisible hand, guided by personal interests and rationality, people make decisions that have a positive impact on the economy as a whole.

The best interests of society are achieved through freedom of production and freedom of consumption. The constant interaction of individual factors of pressure on market supply and demand leads to natural movements in prices and trade flows. Economists who believe in the invisible hand theory have lobbied for less government intervention and more free market opportunities for exchange.

Advantages and Disadvantages of Rational Choice Theory

Many economists question the validity of rational choice theory and the invisible hand theory. Opponents note that people do not always make rational decisions aimed at maximising utility. The field of behavioural economics is the latest intervention in the problem of explaining the economic decision-making processes of individuals and institutions.

Behavioural economics attempts to explain from a psychological point of view why individual actors sometimes make irrational decisions and why and how their behaviour does not always match the predictions of economic models. Critics of rational choice theory say that, of course, in an ideal world, people will always make the optimal decisions that bring them the greatest benefit and satisfaction. However, we do not live in an ideal world. In fact, people are often driven by emotions and external factors.

Nobel laureate Herbert Simon rejected the assumption of perfect rationality in mainstream economics and instead proposed a theory of bounded rationality. The theory states that people do not always have access to all the information they need to make the best decisions. Simon argues that for most decisions people make, it is almost impossible to know all the alternatives or all the consequences of each alternative.

Similarly, economist Richard Taylor points out further limitations to the assumption that people act as rational actors. Thaler's mental accounting philosophy shows that people value some dollars more than others, even if all dollars have the same value.

They may go to another store to buy $20 to save $10, but they won't go to another store to buy $1,000 to save $10.

Like all theories, one of the advantages of rational choice theory is that it helps explain individual and collective behavior. All theories try to give meaning to what we observe in the world. Rational choice theory can explain why individuals, groups, and society as a whole make specific choices based on specific costs and rewards.

Rational choice theory also helps explain seemingly irrational behavior. Since the central premise of rational choice theory is that all actions are rational, any action can be censored because of its underlying rational motives.

Pros of Rational Choice Theory

Helps explain individual and collective behavior.

All theories try to give meaning to what we observe in the world.

Can help explain seemingly irrational behavior.

Cons of Rational Choice Theory

People don't always make rational decisions.

In reality, people are often driven by irrational external factors such as emotions.

People don't have perfect access to the information they need to make the most rational decision every time.

People value some dollars more than others.

Examples of rational choice theory

According to rational choice theory, rational investors are those who will quickly buy any undervalued stock and sell any overvalued one.

An example of a rational consumer is a person choosing between two cars. Car B is cheaper than car A, so the consumer buys car B.

Although rational choice theory is logical and easy to understand, in the real world it typically contradicts itself. For example, the political faction that supported the Brexit referendum on 23 June 2016

Use stocks based on sentiment, not rational analysis. These movements led to a semi-shocking and unexpected vote—the official decision of the UK to leave the EU. Financial markets then reacted with shock, sharply increasing short-term volatility as measured by the CBOE Volatility Index (VIX).

CHAPTER NINETEEN

SCARCITY OR DEFICIT

What is the main reason for the shortage?

The main causes of economic deficits are demand, supply and structural factors. Demand induction is when supply stays constant while demand increases. Supply-induced is when the supply of a resource is lower than demand, and structural is when one part of the population cannot get as much of a resource as another.

What does a deficit / scarcity mean in an economy?

Scarcity in an economy means that the demand for a resource exceeds the supply of that resource because the resource is finite. Scarcity results in consumers having to decide how best to allocate resources to meet all basic needs and as much as possible.

What is the difference between relative rarity and absolute rarity?

Relative scarcity means that the supply of a resource is naturally limited. This is not because companies are not creating enough resources, but rather because there is only a certain amount of available resources on the planet. However, relative scarcity also refers to the ratio of supply to demand. For example, oil. Although oil is plentiful now, the amount available is limited and at some point it will not be able to meet the demand. This is relatively small. Absolute rarity also means that resources are naturally limited, but not related to demand. The best example is time. 24 hours a day, 7 days a week, 52 weeks a year. There is very little time

How does society deal with scarcity?

A society can cope with the deficit by increasing the supply. The more goods and services available to everyone, the smaller the shortage. Of course, there are also limits to increasing supply, such as capacity, available land, time, etc. Another way to deal with shortages is to reduce demand. The lower the demand or need for certain non-essential goods and services, such as food and housing, the lower the pressure on scarce resources.

What is a deficit?

Scarcity refers to a fundamental economic problem—the gap between a finite resource and theoretically infinite demand. This situation requires people to make a decision about how to allocate resources efficiently to meet basic needs and as many additional needs as possible. Any resource with a non-zero consumption cost is scarce to some extent, but in practice, relative scarcity matters.

Deficiency is also known as "deficiency".

- Scarcity refers to the limited and costly means to an end.
- Scarcity is at the heart of the fundamental problem of economics: the allocation of limited resources to meet unlimited needs.
- Even free natural resources can become scarce if the cost of acquiring or consuming natural resources rises, or if consumer demand for previously undesirable resources rises due to changes in preferences or new uses.

Understanding Scarcity

The British economist Lionel Robbins, in his 1932 Essay on the Nature and Significance of Economics, used scarcity to define the discipline:

In a hypothetical world where every resource — water, hand sanitizer, expert translations of Hittite inscriptions, enriched uranium, organic cabbage, bourbon — is plentiful, there would be nothing for economists to study. There is no need to make decisions about how to allocate resources, and no need to weigh research and quantification. On the other hand, in the real world, you have to pay for everything. In other words, every resource is scarce to some extent.

Money and time are usually scarce resources. Most people have too little of one, the other, or both. The unemployed may have plenty of time, but find it difficult to pay rent due to lack of funds. On the other hand, an ardent executive may have the financial means to retire on a whim, but are forced to eat ten-minute meals and sleep four hours a night: they have a lot of money, but they do not have enough time.

The third category has neither time nor money. Wealthy people are rarely seen in the wild.

Natural Resource Scarcity

Natural resources can go beyond scarcity for two reasons. Anything that can be consumed at zero cost or traded for an almost unlimited supply of other goods is not scarce. Or, if consumers are indifferent to a resource, have no desire to consume it, or are completely unaware of it or its potential use, then it is not scarce, even if the total existing quantity is clearly limited. However, even resources are considered infinitely abundant, and since they are free in dollar terms, they can become scarce in a sense.

Take air as an example. From a personal point of view, breathing is completely free. However, there are many costs associated with the activity. This requires breathable air, which has become increasingly difficult to take for granted since the industrial revolution. Today, in many cities, poor air quality is associated with high morbidity and mortality. To avoid these costly cases and ensure the safe breathing of citizens, governments, or utilities must invest in electricity generation methods that do not produce harmful emissions. This may be more expensive than the dirtier methods, but even if they are not, they require a significant capital outlay. These costs are borne by citizens in one way or another. In other words, free breathing is not free.

If the government decides to allocate resources to make the air clean enough to breathe, there will be many problems. What are some ways to improve air quality? What is most effective in the short, medium and long term? How cost-effective? How should quality and cost be balanced? What are the trade-offs of different options? Where should the money come from? Should the government raise taxes? If so, what is the object of the tax increase? Will the government borrow money? Will you print money? How will the government keep track of its costs, liabilities, and benefits from projects (i.e., accounting)?

Soon, the scarcity of clean air (the cost of clean air is not zero) raised many questions about how to allocate resources efficiently. Scarcity is the fundamental problem that gives rise to the economy.

CHAPTER TWENTY

ASSUMES OR CETERIS PARIBUS

What are Cithers Paribus?

Ceteris paribus, literally "keep the rest unchanged," is a Latin phrase that is usually translated into English as "everything else is the same." A prevailing assumption in mainstream economic thought that serves as a concise indication of the influence of one economic variable on another, provided that all other variables remain constant.

- Ceteris paribus is a Latin phrase that usually means "ceteris paribus".
- In economics, it serves as a shorthand for the influence of one economic variable on another, provided that all other variables remain constant.
- Many economists rely, other things being equal, on describing the relative trends of markets and on building and testing economic models.
- The difficulty, ceteris paribus, is to keep all other variables constant in order to isolate the factors causing the change.

- In fact, one can never assume that "ceteris paribus".

Understanding Ceteris Paribus

In economics and finance, when discussing causal relationships, it is often used ceteris paribus. Economists might say that raising the minimum wage will increase unemployment, that an increase in the money supply will lead to inflation, that lowering marginal cost will increase a company's economic profit, or that passing laws to control rents in cities will reduce the supply of affordable housing. Of course, many factors can influence these results, but other things being equal, you can leave all other factors constant and focus on the influence of only one factor.

The hypothesis of Ceteris paribus helps transform deductive social science into a methodologically positive "exact" science. It creates an imaginary system of rules and conditions according to which economists can pursue certain goals. In other words, it helps economists get around the problems of human nature and limited knowledge.

Most, though not all, economists build and test economic models, other things being equal. In simple terms, this means that economists can leave all the variables in the model the same and change them all at once. Other things being equal, there are limitations, especially when these arguments contradict each other. However, it is an important and useful way of describing the relative trend of the market.

Applications of Ceteris Paribus

Suppose you want to explain the price of milk. If you think about it a bit, the cost of milk is clearly influenced by many factors: the availability of cows, their health, the cost of keeping cows, the amount of land available, the cost of possible milk alternatives, the number of milk suppliers, the economic inflation rate, consumer preferences, transportation, and many other variables. So one economist turned to ceteris paribus, which essentially says that if all other factors remain the same, such as a decrease in the supply of productive cows, the price of milk will rise.

As another example, take the law of supply and demand. Economists say that the law of demand shows that more goods tend to be bought at lower prices, other things being equal. Alternatively, if the demand for any given product exceeds the supply of the product, other things being equal, the price may rise.

Ceteris paribus is an extension of scientific modelling. The scientific method is based on identifying, isolating and testing the influence of independent variables on dependent variables.

History of Ceteris Paribus

Two major publications helped transform mainstream economics from deductive social science based on logical observation and deduction to empirical positivist natural science. The first was Léon Walras' Elements of Pure Economics, published in 1874, which introduced the theory of general equilibrium.

The second is John Maynard Keynes' General Theory of Employment, Interest and Money, first published in 1936 and pioneering modern macroeconomics.

To be more like the academically respected "exact sciences" of physics and chemistry, economics began to make heavy use of mathematics. However, variable uncertainty is a major problem. Economics cannot isolate the controlled and independent variables of a mathematical equation. There are also problems with applying the scientific method, which isolates specific variables and tests their relationship to confirm or disprove hypotheses.

Economics, of course, is not suitable for testing scientific hypotheses. In the field of epistemology, scientists may learn through logical thought experiments, also called deduction, or through empirical observation and testing, also called positivism. Geometry is the science of logical inference. Physics is an empirical science.

Unfortunately, economics and the scientific method are naturally incompatible. No economist is able to control all the participants in economic activity, keep their behaviour unchanged, and then conduct a certain test. No single economist can even identify all the key variables in a given economy. For any given economic event, there may be tens or hundreds of potential explanatory variables.

Enter other conditions without changes. Mainstream economists build abstract models in which they pretend that all variables stay the same except for the variable they want to test. This style of pretence, other things being equal, is the key to general equilibrium theory.

As the economist Milton Friedman wrote in 1953, "a theory is judged by its predictive power with respect to the class of phenomena to be 'explained'."

Assuming that all but one of the variables remain constant, economists can translate relatively deductive market trends into perfectly controllable mathematical progressions. Human nature has been replaced by balanced equations.

Benefits of Ceteris Paribus

Suppose an economist wants to show that the minimum wage causes unemployment and free money causes inflation. There was no way they could build two identical test economies and introduce minimum wage laws or start printing dollar bills.

Therefore, active economists charged with testing their theories must create an appropriate foundation for the scientific method, even if that means making wildly unrealistic assumptions. Economists assume that buyers and sellers are price takers rather than price makers.

Economists also assume that participants have complete information about their choices, since any indecisiveness or bad decisions based on incomplete information can create holes in the model. A model created in the economy, all other things being equal, seems to make accurate predictions in the real world, then the model is considered successful. If the model does not seem to be able to make accurate predictions, it is modified.

This can complicate positive economics: there may be situations where the model seems right today, but not a year later. Some economists reject positivism and accept deduction as the main mechanism of discovery. Most, however, accept the limitations of the ceteris paribus assumption to make the field of economics more like chemistry than philosophy.

Criticism of Ceteris Paribus

The ceteris paribus assumption underlies almost all major microeconomic and macroeconomic models. However, some critics of mainstream economics point out that, other things being equal, economists have reason to ignore real questions about human nature.

Economists admit that these assumptions are highly unrealistic, but these models lead to concepts such as utility curves, cross elasticity, and monopoly. Antitrust law is actually based on the perfect competition argument. The Austrian School of Economics argues that, other things being equal, the hypothesis has gone too far, turning economics from a useful, logical social science into a set of mathematical problems.

Let's go back to the supply and demand example, which is one of my favourite uses of all else being equal. Every introductory microeconomics textbook shows a static supply and demand graph where prices are given to both producers and consumers, that is, at a given price, consumers demand a certain amount and producers offer a certain amount. This is a necessary step, at least within this framework, for the economy to tolerate difficulties in the pricing process.

But price is not a separate entity in the real world of producers and consumers. Instead, consumers and producers themselves set prices based on their subjective assessment of the respective product and the amount of money sold.

This supply and demand structure is "out of touch with reality," writes financial consultant Frank Szostak.

He argues that instead of dealing with equilibrium situations, students should first learn how prices arise. He argues that any subsequent conclusions or public policy drawn from these abstract graphic images are inevitably wrong.

Like prices, many other factors that affect the economy or finances are constantly changing. Independent research or testing may authorize use, other things being equal. But one should never really assume that "ceteris paribus" is something like the stock market. There are so many factors that impact stock prices that can change all the time, and you can't pick just one.

Ceteris Paribus vs Mutatis Mutandis

Despite some similarities in terms of assumptions, ceteris paribus should not be confused with mutatis mutandis, which translates as "after making the necessary changes." It is used to recognize that comparisons of, for example, two variables require some necessary changes that are not specified due to their obviousness.

On the contrary, ceteris paribus, any and all options other than those expressly stated are excluded. In particular, when talking about the counterfactual, the phrase mutatis mutandis is often used as a shorthand for original and derivative changes that have been discussed before or considered obvious.

The ultimate difference between these two opposing principles comes down to correlation and causation. The principle of ceteris paribus helps to study the causal influence of one variable on another. Conversely, the principle of contrast helps to analyse the correlation between the influence of one variable on another and the arbitrary change in other variables.

What is Ceteris Paribus in Economics?

Other things being equal, in economics it is about how an isolated variable changes the economic environment, assuming that all other variables remain constant. In economics, ceteris paribus, they usually take on very great importance, since national economic and macroeconomic conditions are very complex. However, ceteris paribus, it is the practice of observing how one economic concept (such as inflation) affects broader concepts.

What is an example of ceteris paribus in economics?

Other things being equal, people will buy less milk if the price of milk rises. This hypothesis ignores how other alternatives behave, how household income behaves, or non-economic factors such as the health benefits of milk. Other things being equal, people will buy less if the price is higher.

Is Ceteris Paribus a law?

Other things being equal, it is considered a natural right. It is not codified by any government; rather, it is thought to occur naturally depending on how certain variables interact. For example, if the US produced more oil at home, gasoline inventories would increase and natural gas prices would decrease. There are no legal requirements for this; it is simply assumed that this is a consequence of the natural course of the situation.

What helps to find Ceteris Paribus?

Other things being equal, it helps to determine which variables affect the results. By holding one variable constant, or by assuming that only one variable changes, one can conclude that any relevant change is directly related to that single variable. Ceteris paribus can help manage indicators of customer tastes and preferences, consumer spending, commodity prices, market expectations or government policies.

The bottom lines

Other things being equal, this is a broad term that defines which variables change and which remain unchanged in a given situation. Often, to isolate a variable, economists refer to ceteris paribus to make it clear that their assumptions about a given outcome are only correct if all other variables remain constant. While this is indeed unlikely, other things being equal, due to the complexity of macroeconomic factors, it can still be useful in testing variables and determining what caused the results.

CHAPTER TWENTY-ONE

RATIONAL PERSON OR RATIONAL BEHAVIOR

What is rational behavior?

Rational behavior refers to a decision-making process based on choices that results in an individual's best interests or level of utility. The assumption of rational behaviours means that people are more likely to take actions that benefit them than actions that neutralize or harm them. Most classical economic theories are based on the assumption that all people involved in an activity act rationally.

- Rational behaviours refers to a decision-making process based on choices that provide the best level of benefit or utility.
- Rational choice theory is an economic theory that assumes rational behavior of people.

- Rational behavior may not involve obtaining the greatest monetary or material benefit, since the satisfaction received may be purely emotional or non-monetary.

Understand rational behaviors

Rational behaviours is the cornerstone of rational choice theory, an economic theory that assumes that people always make decisions that provide them with the highest personal utility. These decisions provide the greatest benefit or satisfaction to people, given the options available. Rational behaviours may not involve obtaining the greatest monetary or material benefit, since the satisfaction received may be purely emotional or non-monetary.

For example, while it may be financially more beneficial for an executive to stay with the company rather than retire early, if they feel that the benefits of retirement outweigh the utility, it is still considered rational for them to seek early retirement. She received a salary. A person's best interests may include non-monetary returns.

In addition, a person's willingness to take risks or, conversely, his risk aversion can be considered rational, depending on his goals and circumstances. For example, an investor may decide to take on more risk in his retirement account than in his college account. Both would be considered rational choices for that investor.

Behavioral economics

Behavioural economics is a method of economic analysis that considers psychological data to explain human behaviours in relation to economic decision-making. According to rational choice theory, rational people have the ability to control themselves and are not affected by emotional factors. However, behavioural economics recognizes that people are emotional and easily distracted, and as a result, their behavior does not always match the predictions of economic models. Psychological factors and emotions can influence a person's behavior and push him to make decisions that seem not entirely rational.

Behavioral economics attempts to explain why people make certain decisions, such as how much a cup of coffee costs, whether to continue with college or a healthy lifestyle, and how much to save for retirement, and other decisions that most people have to make as children. Some point in their lives.

Investors can also make decisions based primarily on sentiment, such as investing in companies that investors view favorably, even if the financial models suggest the investment is not wise.

Example of rational behavior

For example, if a person strongly believes in the value of organic products, they may choose to invest in stocks of organic food businesses rather than in traditional manufacturing operations. They can do this regardless of the current value of the organic business versus the traditional business, although the traditional business will generate higher returns.

CHAPTER TWENTY-TWO

HEURISTICS

What is a heuristic?

A heuristic or heuristic method is any method of problem-solving that uses practical methods or various shortcuts to arrive at a solution that may not be optimal but sufficient for a limited time period or deadline.

Heuristics are designed to be flexible and used for making quick decisions, especially when finding a better solution is not possible or practical, and when dealing with complex data. These cognitive labels feature prominently in behavioral economics.

- A heuristic is a method of solving a problem quickly enough to provide useful results in a limited amount of time.
- Investors and financial professionals use heuristics to speed up analysis and investment decisions.
- Heuristics can lead to bad decisions based on limited datasets, but decision speed can sometimes make up for the shortcomings.

- Behavioral economics focuses on heuristics as limiting people to behave like rational actors.
- Availability, anchoring, confirmation bias, and hot hand fallacy are some examples of heuristics that people use in economic life.

Understanding heuristics

Various inventions and innovations in digital technology have changed every aspect of many industries, including finance, retail, media, and transportation. Some daily activities are obsolete; for example, depositing checks into a bank account without visiting a local branch, buying groceries and services online, and delivering takeaway food through a food delivery app.

All of these new technologies are creating data that is increasingly being used across many industries and sectors. Professionals in any industry can work with large amounts of complex data to solve problems. When time and resources are limited, heuristics can be used to solve the problem of data complexity.

Advantages and disadvantages of using heuristics

Heuristics help you make timely decisions. Analysts in every industry use rules of thumb such as reasonable guessing, trial and error, elimination processes, past formulas, and analysis of historical data to solve problems. Heuristics simplify and speed up decision-making through shortcuts and reasonably good calculations.

The use of heuristics involves trade-offs that make the method prone to bias and errors in judgment. The user's final decision may not be the optimal or optimal solution. Or the decisions made may be inaccurate, and the data selected may not be sufficient (resulting in inaccurate solutions to the problem). For example, imitator investors often mimic the investment models of successful investment managers to avoid doing their own research on securities and the quantitative and qualitative information associated with them.

Heuristic example

Representativeness

A popular method of quick problem-solving identified in behavioral economics is called representational heuristics. Representation uses mental shortcuts to make decisions based on past events or characteristics that represent or resemble the current situation. ABC fast food, for example, has spread to India and its stock has skyrocketed. One analyst noted that India is a profitable business for all fast food chains. So when fast food company XYZ announced plans to expand in India next year, analysts immediately gave XYZ a 'buy' recommendation.

While his label saved both companies from looking at the data, it may not have been the best decision. Research shows that fast food XYZ food may not appeal to Indian consumers.

Anchoring and Adjustment

Anchoring and Adjustment is another popular heuristic. With anchoring and adjusting, a person starts with a specific target number or value, called an anchor point, and then adjusts that number until an acceptable value is reached over time. The main problem with this approach is that if the anchor's initial value is not the true value, all subsequent adjustments will systematically deviate the anchor from the true value.

Heuristics and psychology

Heuristics were first identified and taken seriously by scholars in the mid-20th century in the work of Herbert Simon, who questioned why individuals and corporations do not behave as rational entities in the real world, even when market pressures punish irrational decisions. Simon found that business managers often do not optimize, but rely on a set of heuristics for "satisfaction" (a combination of the words "satisfied" and "enough"), that is, they use a set of shortcuts quite well performed.

According to Simon, due to the biological limitations of the human mind, people cannot consistently calculate and process all the information at their disposal. So one may want to act rationally, but be bound by these constraints—what he called bounded rationality.

Later, in the 1970s and 1980s, Amos Tversky and Daniel Kahneman, while working at the Hebrew University of Jerusalem, developed the so-called prospect theory based on the work of Herbert Simon. As a cornerstone of behavioral economics, prospect theory outlines several heuristics that people subconsciously use when making financial estimates. The main takeaway is that people are loss averse—the losses are greater than the gains (i.e., the pain of losing $50 is much greater than the joy of gaining $50). This is where people use heuristics to avoid implementation losses, which sometimes encourages them to take too much risk, but often leads to big losses.

More recently, behavioral economists have attempted to develop policies, or "nudges," to help correct people's irrational use of heuristics to help them achieve more optimal outcomes. For example, by allowing people to opt out of default retirement savings plans instead of opting in.

What are the types of heuristics?

To date, behavioral economics has identified many heuristics or developed some heuristics to help people make difficult decisions. In behavioral economics, representation, anchoring and adjustment, and accessibility (novelty) are most frequently mentioned. Heuristics can be classified in many ways, such as cognitive biases versus emotional biases, or judgmental versus computational biases.

What is heuristic thinking?

Heuristic thinking uses mental shortcuts—often unconsciously—to make complex decisions or judgments quickly and efficiently. They can be in the form of "rules of thumb" (like setting aside 5% of your income for a comfortable retirement) or cognitive processes that we are largely unaware of, such as affordability bias.

What are computer heuristics?

In computer science, heuristics refers to a method of solving a problem that has proven to be faster or more efficient than traditional methods. This may include using approximations rather than exact calculations, or using methods that bypass other computationally intensive procedures.

CHAPTER TWENTY-THREE

ANCHORING AND ADJUSTMENT

What is anchoring and adjustment?

Anchoring and accommodation is the phenomenon in which people base their initial thoughts and reactions on one point of information and use that starting point to make changes. Anchor-and-adjust heuristic describes the situation where a person uses a certain target number or value as a starting point (called an anchor point) and then adjusts that information until an acceptable value is reached over time. Often these adjustments are not enough and too close to the original anchor, which is a problem when the anchor is very different from the real answer.

- Anchor and adjust is a cognitive heuristic in which a person starts with an initial idea and adjusts their beliefs based on that starting point.
- Anchoring and tuning can produce erroneous results if the initial anchor point deviates from the true value.
- Awareness of the anchor, monetary incentives, careful consideration of a range of possible ideas, knowledge,

experience, personality, and emotions can all change the effect of the anchor.

- Anchor can be used to gain an advantage in sales and price negotiations, where setting up an initial anchor influences subsequent negotiations in your favor.

Understanding Anchoring and Adjustment

Anchoring is a cognitive bias described by behavioral finance in which people focus on a target number or value—usually the first number or value they receive, such as expected prices or economic forecasts. Unlike the conservative bias, which has a similar effect but is based on how investors relate new information to old information, anchoring occurs when people make new decisions based on old anchoring measures. A comprehensive review of new information to determine its effect on the original prediction or opinion can help mitigate the effects of anchoring and adjustment, but the characteristics of the decision maker are just as important as conscious consideration.

The problem with anchoring and adjusting is that if the anchor's initial value is not the true value, all subsequent adjustments will systematically deviate the anchor from the true value. However, if the anchor point is close to the true value, there is practically no issue.

One problem with adjustments is that they can be affected by irrelevant information that a person might consider and make unreasonable links to actual target values. For example, suppose a person is shown a random number and then asked an unrelated question to be answered in the form of an estimate, or a math equation to be performed quickly. Even if the random number they show has nothing to do with the answer they are looking for, it can be seen as a visual cue and anchor to their answer. Anchor values can be self-generated, based on a pricing model or forecasting tool, or provided by an external party.

Research shows that several factors can influence tethering, but it's hard to avoid even if people are aware of it and intentionally avoid it. In experimental studies, telling people about pegging, warning them that it may impact their judgment, and even giving them a monetary incentive to avoid pegging can reduce, but not eliminate, the effects of pegging.

A higher level of experience and skill in a particular area can help reduce tethering in that subject area, while higher general cognitive ability can reduce tethering in general. Personality and emotions can also play a role. Depressive mood enhances anchoring, as do personality traits such as good nature, conscientiousness, introversion, and openness.

Anchoring and Adjustment in Business and Finance

Anchoring and adjustment can be a powerful tool in sales, pricing, and wage negotiations. Research shows that setting an anchor at the start of a negotiation has a greater impact on the outcome than intervening in the negotiation process. Setting a thoughtful starting point affects the range of all subsequent counteroffers.

For example, a used car dealer (or any seller) may offer a very high price to start negotiations, which may be much higher than fair value. Since the high price is the anchor, the final price is usually higher than what the car dealer offered to start at a fair or low price. Similar techniques can be applied to hiring negotiations when a hiring manager or potential employee offers a starting salary. Either side can then push the discussion towards that starting point, hoping to reach an acceptable amount from the anchor.

In finance, the results of pricing models or economic forecasting tools can be a starting point for analysts. One possible way to counteract this is to consider several different models or chains of evidence. Social psychology researcher Philip Tetlock found that forecasters who made predictions based on many different ideas or perspectives ("foxes") tended to make more accurate predictions than those who focused on one model or a few big ideas ("hedgehogs"). ").

Considering several different models and a number of different forecasts can make the analyst's job less prone to anchoring.

CHAPTER TWENTY-FOUR

GAME THEORY

What is game theory?

Game theory is a theoretical framework for representing social situations between competing players. In a sense, game theory is the science of strategy, or at least of optimal decision-making by independent and competitive players in a strategic environment.

Game theory is a theoretical framework for representing social situations between competing players and making optimal decisions for independent and competing players in a strategic setting.

Using game theory, you can develop realistic scenarios for situations like price competition and product launches (and more) and predict their outcomes.

Scenarios include Prisoner's Dilemma and Dictator Games, among others.

How Game Theory Works

The main pioneers of game theory were the mathematician John von Neumann and the economist Oscar Morgenstern in the 1940s.

Many consider the mathematician John Nash to have made the first important continuation of the work of von Neumann and Morgenstern.

Game theory focuses on games that are models of interactive situations between rational players. The essence of game theory is that the payoff of one player depends on the strategy implemented by the other player.

The game recognizes the player's personality, preferences, and available strategies, as well as how these strategies affect the outcome. Depending on the model, various other requirements or assumptions may be required.

Game theory has a wide range of applications, including psychology, evolutionary biology, military science, politics, economics, and business. Despite numerous achievements, game theory is still a young and developing science.

Definition of game theory

Whenever we are faced with a situation involving two or more players with known payoffs or measurable consequences, we can use game theory to determine the most likely outcome. Let's first define some terms commonly used in game theory research:

- **Game**: any set of situations in which the outcome depends on the actions of two or more decision makers (players).
- **Players**: strategic decision makers in the context of games
- **Strategy**: The overall plan of action that the player will take given a number of situations that may arise in the game.

- **Payout**: A payout that a player receives for achieving a certain result (the payout can be in any measurable form, from dollars to utility).
- **Information set**: information available at the current moment of the game (the term information set is most often used when the game consists of sequential components).
- **Equilibrium**: The point in the game where both sides make a decision and reach a result.

The Nash equilibrium

The Nash equilibrium is the result achieved, which, once reached, means that no player can unilaterally change their decisions in order to increase their profit. It can also be considered "no regrets" because once the decision is made, the player will not regret the decision given the consequences.

In most cases, Nash equilibrium is reached over time. However, once the Nash equilibrium is reached, there is no deviation. Now that we have learned how to find the Nash equilibrium, let's see how a one-way action will affect the situation. Does it make sense? It doesn't have to be that way, which is why "Nash Equilibrium" is described as "no regrets". In general, there can be more than one equilibrium in a game.

However, this usually occurs in games with more complex elements than two-player selection. In a simultaneous game repeated over time, after some trial and error, one of these multiple equilibria is reached. This situation of working overtime to select different options until a balance is reached is most common in the business world, where two companies are evaluating a highly interchangeable product, such as an airline ticket or a soft drink.

Impact on the economy and business

Game theory revolutionized economics by solving key problems of previous mathematical economic models. For example, neoclassical economics has difficulty understanding the expectations of entrepreneurs and cannot cope with imperfect competition. Game theory shifts its focus from established equilibrium to market processes.

In business, game theory helps to model the competitive behavior of economic agents. Businesses often have multiple strategic options that affect their ability to capture economic benefits.

For example, a business may face dilemmas such as abandoning an existing product or developing a new one, cutting prices compared to competitors, or adopting new marketing strategies. Economists typically use game theory to understand the behavior of oligopolistic firms. It helps predict the likely outcomes of companies engaging in certain activities such as pricing and collusion.

Types of game theory

While there are many types of game theory (e.g. symmetric/asymmetric, simultaneous/sequential, etc.), the most common are cooperative and non-cooperative game theories. Cooperative game theory deals with how coalitions or cooperative groups interact when only the payoff is known. It is a game between players' alliances, not individuals, and it asks how groups are formed and how they distribute profits among the players.

Non-cooperative game theory deals with how rational economic agents trade with each other to achieve their goals. The most common non-cooperative game is the strategy game, which lists only the available strategies and combinations of options. A simple example of a real non-cooperative game is rock-paper-scissors.

Example from game theory

Game theory analyzes several "games". Below, we briefly describe some of them.

The Prisoner's Dilemma

The prisoner's dilemma is the most famous example of game theory. Consider the example of two criminals arrested for a crime. Prosecutors do not have hard evidence to convict them. However, in order to get a confession of guilt, officials took the prisoners out of separate cells and interrogated everyone in a separate room. None of the prisoners could communicate with each other. The officials showed four deals, usually presented as 2 x 2 boxes.

If both plead guilty, they will each be sentenced to five years in prison.

If Prisoner 1 pleads guilty but Prisoner 2 does not, Prisoner 1 will be sentenced to 3 years and Prisoner 2 to 9 years.

If Prisoner 2 pleads guilty and Prisoner 1 does not, Prisoner 1 will be sentenced to 10 years and Prisoner 2 to two years.

If neither side pleads guilty, each will be imprisoned for two years.

The most profitable strategy is to deny it. However, neither side knows the tactics of the other and is not sure that one of them will not plead guilty, and both can plead guilty and be sentenced to five years in prison. The Nash equilibrium states that in a prisoner's dilemma, both parties will take actions that are best for them individually, but not for them collectively.

The expression "an eye for an eye" or "tit-for-tat" has been identified as the best strategy for optimizing the prisoner's dilemma. An eye for an eye was proposed by Anatoly Rapoport, who developed a strategy in which each participant in the repeated prisoner's dilemma adheres to a course of action consistent with the opponent's previous move. For example, if provoked, the players will retaliate, if not provoked, the players will cooperate.

Dictator game

This is a simple game in which player A must decide how to distribute the prize money to player B, and player B has no opinion on player A's decision. Although this is not a game-theoretic strategy per se, it provides some interesting insights into human behavior. The experiment showed that about 50% kept all the money for themselves, 5% divided it equally, and another 45% gave other participants a smaller share.

The game of dictator is closely related to the game of ultimatum, in which player A receives a certain amount of money, part of which must be given to player B, an amount that player B can accept or refuse. The problem is that if the second player refuses the amount offered, then both A and B get nothing. Dictators and the ultimatum game provide important lessons on issues such as charity and philanthropy.

The Volunteer's Dilemma

In the plight of volunteers, someone has to take over the housework or work for the common good. If no one volunteers, the worst will be achieved. Take, for example, a company with rampant accounting fraud, even if upper management is unaware of it. Some junior members of the accounting department were aware of the fraud but were reluctant to report it to senior management as it could lead to the dismissal of employees involved in the fraud and likely prosecution.

Being named a whistleblower can also have some repercussions. But if no one volunteers, massive fraud could lead to companies eventually going bankrupt and everyone losing their jobs.

The Centipede games

The game of centipede is a broad form of game theory in which two players alternately have the chance to win a large share of a slowly growing sum of money. This is arranged so that if the player passes the stash to his opponent, who then takes the stash, the player receives less money than if he took the pot.

The centipede game ends when a player takes the stash, that player gets the larger part and the other player gets the smaller part. The game has a predetermined total number of rounds, and each player knows these rounds in advance.

Limitations of game theory

The biggest problem with game theory is that, like most other economic models, it is based on the assumption that people are rational self-interested actors who seek to maximize utility. Of course, we are social beings who cooperate and care for the well-being of others, often at our own expense. Game theory cannot explain the fact that in some cases we can get into a Nash equilibrium and in others not, depending on the social context and the players.

What game is played in game theory?

It is called game theory because the theory attempts to understand the strategic actions of two or more "players" in a given situation involving set rules and outcomes. Although game theory is used in several disciplines, it is most commonly used as a tool in business and economics studies. The "game" may include how two competing companies will react to the other's price cuts, whether one company should buy the other, or how stock market traders react to price changes. Theoretically, these games can be divided into the prisoner's dilemma, the games of the dictator, the eagle and the dove, Bach or Stravinsky.

What are the assumptions about these games?

Like many economic models, game theory contains a strict set of assumptions that must remain theoretical in order to make good predictions in practice. First, all players are rational utility-maximizing players who have complete information about the game, the rules, and the consequences. Players are not allowed to communicate or interact with each other. Possible outcomes are not only known in advance, but cannot be changed. Theoretically, the number of players in a game can be unlimited, but most games will only have two players.

What is Nash equilibrium?

Nash equilibrium is an important concept relating to a steady state in a game where no player can gain an advantage by unilaterally changing their strategies, assuming the other players have not changed their strategies either. Nash's equilibria provide a concept for solutions in non-cooperative (competitive) games. It is named after John Nash, who received the Nobel Prize for his work in 1994.

Who Invented Game Theory?

Game theory owes much to the work of mathematician John von Neumann and economist Oscar Morgenstern in the 1940s, and was developed extensively by many other researchers and scientists in the 1950s.

It remains an active area of research and applied science to this day.

CHAPTER TWENTY-FIVE

ECONOMIST

What is an economist?

Economists are experts who study the relationship between a society's resources and their production or output. Economists study societies ranging from small local communities to entire nations and even the global economy.

Economists' expert opinions and research are used to shape a variety of policies, including interest rates, tax laws, employment programs, international trade agreements, and corporate strategies.

An economist is an expert who studies the relationship between a society's resources and their production or output, using many indicators to predict future trends.

In 2021, economists will earn an average salary of $105,630 a year, or $50.79 an hour, according to the U.S. Bureau of Labor Statistics.

There are two basic requirements for a career in economics: an advanced degree, such as a doctoral degree. Or a master's degree, as well as a research-oriented area of specialization.

Economists' theories can provide businesses and governments with the ability to respond to the future direction of the economy.

Economists perform many tasks: research economic issues, conduct surveys and collect data, analyze data using mathematical models, statistical methods and software, present research results in reports, tables and graphs, interpret and predict market trends, advise businesses and governments. And individuals; advise on economic issues; write articles for academic journals and other media.

In 2021, economists will earn an average salary of $105,630 a year, or $50.79 an hour, according to the U.S. Bureau of Labor Statistics.

Meet the Economists

There is a good chance that someone interested in a career in economics will work in government. According to the US Bureau of Labor Statistics, about 36 percent of economists work for federal or state agencies. Economists also serve as professors in corporations or economic think tanks.

There are two main requirements for a career in economics. First, economists often have advanced degrees, such as PhDs. or a master's degree. The typical initial education for an economist is a master's degree. Second, economists often develop a field of expertise to focus on their research work.

Economists influence strategic economic plans

Economists are responsible for analyzing data that includes economic indicators such as gross domestic product and consumer confidence surveys. Economists may study the distribution, availability, and volume of goods and services to determine underlying trends or make economic forecasts.

The work of an economist may be commissioned in a specific area or topic requiring expert evaluation. This can be used for budgeting and planning, where the economist's findings form the basis for an action plan. For example, if spending trends in a particular industry are changing, investors and companies in that industry can turn to economists to see what's next for the market.

In addition, the contributions of economists can reveal the root causes of market cycles. As specific areas of the economy grow, economists' findings may also shape projections of labor market growth.

Economists can turn to a number of factors and elements to gain new insights into what drives trends. Estimates provided by economists can be time-consuming and use a lot of data. Their theory can also empower others to respond to the future direction of the economy. Companies may use this information to adjust their strategies, including whether to continue developing a particular product or whether to abandon a product in favor of a different approach.

CHAPTER TWENTY-SIX

POSITIVE ECONOMICS

What is positive economics?

The term "*positive economics*" refers to objective analysis in economic research. Most economists look at what has already happened and what is currently happening in a given economy to form the basis of their projections for the future. This research process is positive economics. In contrast, normative economic studies base future forecasts on value judgments.

- Positive economics is an objective stream of economics that relies on facts or what is happening.
- Conclusions drawn from a positive economic analysis can be tested and supported by data.
- Empirical economic theory does not give advice or guidance.
- Statements based on normative economics include value judgments or what the future should be.

- Positive economics and normative economics can go hand in hand in policy formulation.

Understanding positive economics

The cornerstone of good economic practice is the study of fact-based behavioral finance or economic relationships and causal interactions for the development of economic theory. Behavioral economics follows the premise, based in psychology, that people will make rational financial choices based on the information they find around them.

Many refer to this study as what-is-economics because it uses fact-based mental decisions. Therefore, normative economics is known as the study of " what should be" or " what should be".

History of positive economics

The history of positive economics dates back to the 19th century. It was during this time that early economists such as John Neville Keynes and John Stuart Mill first developed the concepts of "what is" and "ought to be".

Keynes believed that economic research required logic and methodology, and Mill was an economist who combined economics and philosophy.

Mill studies economics in terms of data (such as supply and demand) rather than values.

These early economists developed theories to support their economic observations. They use evidence from economic conditions to justify these theories.

These ideas were later adopted by modern economists such as Milton Friedman. Friedman is considered one of the most influential economists of the 20th century. He strongly believed in the system of free market capitalism, and his theory became known as monetarism. Friedman was a vocal opponent of monetary policy, saying that it played a major role in the Great Depression.

Testing Positive Economic Theory

Conclusions drawn from empirical economic analysis can be tested and supported by data.

For example, predictions that more people will save if interest rates rise will be based on positive economic theory because past behavior supports the theory.

This analysis is inherently objective, as opposed to subjective normative statements and theories. Much of the information provided by the media is a combination of positive and normative economic statements or assumptions.

Empirical economic theory can help politicians realize normative value judgments. For example, it can describe how the government affects inflation by printing more money, and this statement can be supported by facts and analysis of the behavioral relationships between inflation and money supply growth. But it does not say how to properly set and follow a specific policy on inflation and money printing.

When studied together, both positive and normative economics provide a clear picture of public policy. These theories cover factual and true facts and statements combined with opinion-based analysis. When making political decisions, it is best to understand the positive economic context of behavioral finance and why things happen, because you include normative value judgments about why things happen.

Advantages and Disadvantages of Positive Economics

Positive economics has clear advantages and disadvantages. Here we list some main advantages and disadvantages of this school of economics.

Advantage:

Positive economics is based on objective data, not on opinions and value judgments. We have facts to support any of our claims.

For example, we may use historical data to determine the relationship between interest rates and consumer behavior. Higher interest rates cause consumers to stop borrowing because it means they have to spend more on interest.

Since it is based only on facts and data, there are no value judgments in positive economics. This allows politicians to formulate the appropriate measures necessary to respond to any economic situation in order to move the economy in a certain direction.

for example, the Federal Reserve may cut interest rates to prevent a recession. Personal opinions and feelings can have a significant impact on economic policies and procedures.

For example, people often make decisions based on emotions rather than the facts of their personal financial lives. This can lead people to make the wrong choice. But if they follow the data, they will be able to make more informed decisions through individual economic decisions.

Disadvantages:

Not everyone cares about the fact that certain economic conditions are based on sentiment. As the example above shows, people typically choose to ignore data when making certain decisions. Experts may recommend saving during a weak economy, but people may decide they want to shop big. In fact, it's hard to get emotions out of the economy.

Just because you have a history of data doesn't mean you can come up with a solid solution or conclusion. This is because economics, positive or normative, is not an exact science. There are other considerations that often come into play that can change the results.

Likewise, positive economics cannot be a one-size-fits-all approach. For example, policymakers typically use this data to propose policies or solutions that affect everyone differently. What works for some people does not impact others in the same way. Higher rates could help slow growth, which is good for lenders but bodes ill for borrowers, especially those who are already cash-strapped.

Pros

- Easy to verify as it is based on objective data
- Give politicians more power to make decisions
- Enables people to make smarter choices in their financial and financial lives

Cons

- We can't always separate our emotions from facts.
- Economics is not an exact science, so there are no reliable solutions or conclusions.
- Policies and decisions made by positive economics do not impact everyone equally.

Real examples of positive economy

Go for 15 is a national campaign to promote a $15 minimum wage that will be seen as normative economics.

The position on the $15 minimum wage is a value judgment. Proponents argue that raising the minimum wage is good, while opponents say it is harmful.

There have been many studies on minimum wage increases, but there have been no definitive conclusions to draw broad and comprehensive conclusions about whether minimum wage increases are good or bad. But some details in certain studies can be seen as examples of positive economics.

The Seattle Ordinance

In 2015, Seattle passed a local ordinance to gradually raise the minimum wage for workers in the city. The move means that by 2021 or earlier, all workers will be paid at least $15 an hour, depending on the specific details of the employment. Since then, there have been two major impact studies of the law.

The study, conducted by researchers at the University of California at Berkeley, focused on restaurant employees. Seattle's unemployment rate rose from 5.7% in 2012 to 3.6% in 2016, according to a UC Berkeley study. The average annual salary of a worker has increased by 13.4% over the years.

According to these researchers, fast-food restaurant workers are seeing an increase in their earnings thanks to Seattle's minimum wage increase. This particular data is an example of a positive economy, but the researchers concluded that a higher minimum wage is a success, which is not a positive economy because the research focus is not broad or detailed enough to make such a conclusion.

At the same time, researchers at the University of Washington concluded that the increase in the minimum wage was not successful. But this conclusion is not an example of positive economics. However, some of the specific data they collect will be an example of a positive economy.

For example, they found that when the minimum wage was raised, low-wage workers worked fewer hours. Thus, after the increase in the minimum wage, the total wage of low-income workers decreased by about $125 per month.

The number of low-paid workers fell by 1%, and workers still working were working slightly fewer hours.

While these specific numbers represent a positive economic outlook, the researchers' conclusions remain questionable because other factors not included in the study, such as a potential increase in high-paying jobs, may have influenced the data.

What is positive economics and examples?

Positive economics is an objective analysis of economic research. This includes examining what has happened and what is happening, which allows economists to predict what will happen in the future. A positive economy is tangible, so anything that can be backed up by facts such as inflation, unemployment, housing market statistics, and consumer spending is an example of a positive economy.

What is the difference between positive economics and normative economics?

Positive economics is a branch of economics that relies on objective data, while normative economics is based on subjective information. The latter are based on value judgments based on opinions and personal feelings rather than analysis. Positive economics deals with what is compared to normative economics, which is based on how economic behavior should be.

What are positive and normative statements?

There is a big difference between a positive statement and a normative statement. Positive claims are objective theories that can be tested. On the other hand, normative statements are subjective. They involve the use of opinions and value judgments, and are often based on personal opinions.

What are some examples of normative economics?

Normative economics is represented by everything subjective and value-based. This means that we can use the information we have to say what the future should be like. For example, we may use earnings data to show that a company should pay more taxes. We can form an opinion on the minimum wage with a living wage at the current wage.

The branch of economics called welfare economics deals with normative economics. The leading thinkers in this field were Abram Bergson and Nobel Laureate in Economics Kenneth Arrow.

Bottom line

Economics is considered an art and a science. This is because it combines the use of facts with value judgments. But there are economic flows that separate what is happening now from what is to happen in the future. Positive economics is an objective field of study that draws conclusions from verifiable facts.

On the other hand, normative economics deals with opinions based on these facts. While this may seem like the best option, no society operates with a positive economic stance. In fact, when politicians are developing new solutions, a combination of positive and normative economics may be the best approach.

CHAPTER TWENTY-SEVEN

CONSUMER ECONOMICS

Although a basic understanding of economics is not as important as balancing a family budget or knowing how to drive a car, the forces behind economic research affect every moment of our lives. At its most basic level, economics attempts to explain how and why we make purchasing decisions.

Four key economic concepts – *scarcity, supply and demand, costs and benefits, and incentives* – can help explain many of the decisions people make.

Scarcity explains the fundamental economic problem of having limited or scarce resources in the world to meet seemingly endless needs, a reality that forces people to decide how to allocate resources in the most efficient way.

Due to a lack of resources, people are constantly making choices that depend on their costs and benefits, as well as the incentives provided by different ways of doing things.

Scarcity

Whether you realize it or not, everyone knows something about scarcity because everyone experiences the effects of scarcity. Scarcity explains the fundamental economic problem of having limited or scarce resources in the world to meet seemingly endless needs. This reality forces people to decide how to allocate resources most efficiently to satisfy as many of their highest priorities as possible.

For example, a certain amount of wheat is grown every year. Someone needs bread, someone needs beer. Since wheat is scarce, only a certain amount of this commodity can be produced. How do we decide how much flour to make for bread and beer? One way to solve this problem is a market system driven by supply and demand.

Supply and demand

The market system is driven by supply and demand. Take, for example, beer, if there are many people who want to buy beer, then the demand for beer is considered high. So you can charge more for beer and make more money on average using wheat to make beer than you can be using wheat to make flour.

Hypothetically, this could lead to more people making beer, and after a few production cycles, there will be so much beer on the market – the supply of beer will increase – that beer prices will drop.

While this is an extreme and oversimplified example, at a fundamental level, the concept of supply and demand helps explain why last year's popular products cost half as much as next years.

Costs and benefits

The concepts of costs and benefits are related to the theory of rational choice (and rational expectations) on which economics is based. When economists say that people behave rationally, they mean that people try to maximize the benefit/cost ratio in their decisions.

If the demand for beer is high, breweries will hire more employees to produce more beer, but only if the price of the beer and the amount of beer they sell justify their wages and the materials needed to brew more beer. The extra costs are reasonable. Similarly, consumers will buy the best beer they can afford, but perhaps not the best-tasting beer in the store.

The concepts of costs and benefits apply to decisions other than financial transactions. College students conduct cost-benefit analyzes on a daily basis, choosing certain courses they feel are more important to their success. Sometimes it even means reducing the time they spend studying courses they consider less necessary.

While economics assumes that people are generally rational, many of the decisions' people make are actually very emotional and do not maximize our own interests. For example, advertising exploits people's propensity for irrational behavior. Advertising tries to activate the emotional centers of our brain and tricks us into overestimating the benefits of a particular product.

Everything Is in the Incentives

If you are a parent, boss, teacher, or someone in charge of supervision, you may have been able to offer rewards or incentives to increase the likelihood of a particular outcome.

Economic incentives explain how the action of supply and demand induces producers to produce goods that consumers want, and how consumers conserve scarce resources. When consumer demand for a good increases, the market price of that good increases and producers have an incentive to produce more because they can get a higher price. On the other hand, when a growing shortage of raw materials or means of production for a particular good causes costs to rise and producers reduce supply, the price they charge for the good rises and consumers have an incentive to save that well and keep it at the price they want. Have the most value.

In the brewery example, the owner wants to increase production, so he decides to offer an incentive (bonus) for the shift that produces the most beer in a day. The brewery has two bottle sizes: a 500ml bottle and a 1L bottle. Within a few days, they saw an increase in production from 10,000 to 15,000 bottles per day. The problem is that the incentives they offer are focused not on the number of bottles, but not on the volume of beer. They started getting calls from suppliers asking when orders for liter bottles would come in. By offering a bonus for the number of bottles produced, it becomes profitable for owners to give competing shifts an advantage by only bottling smaller bottles.

When incentives are properly aligned with organizational goals, the benefits can be extraordinary. These methods include profit sharing, performance bonuses, and employee shareholding. However, these incentives can go wrong if the criteria for determining whether the incentives are met do not meet the original goals. Poorly structured performance bonuses, for example, have spurred some executives to take steps to improve their company's financial performance in the short term—just enough to get paid. These measures later proved to be detrimental to the company's long-term health.

Economics Is the Dismal Science

Scarcity is the basis of all economics, the explanation that economics is sometimes called Dismal science. People are constantly making choices that are determined by their costs and benefits. At the individual level, scarcity means that we must make choices based on the incentives that different options give us. At the market level, the impact of the choices made by millions creates the forces of supply and demand.

CHAPTER TWENTY-EIGHT

NORMATIVE ECONOMICS

What is normative economics?

Normative economics is an economic perspective that reflects normative or ideological normative judgments about economic development, investment projects, statements, and scenarios.

Unlike positive economics, which relies on the analysis of objective data, normative economics focuses heavily on value judgments and "what should be" statements rather than facts based on causal statements. It expresses ideological judgments about economic activity that may arise in the event of a change in government policy. Regulatory economic reporting cannot be verified or tested.

- Normative economics seeks to determine what should or should happen.
- Positive economics describes existing economic plans, situations, and conditions, while normative economics seeks to prescribe solutions.

- Normative economics expresses the ideological judgments about economic activity that might arise if there were changes in public policy.
- Behavioral economics tends to be a normative blueprint.
- Normative economics cannot be verified or tested.

Learn about normative economics

Normative economics seeks to determine people's desire or lack of various economic plans, situations, and conditions by asking what should or should happen. As such, normative statements are usually opinion-based analyzes in terms of aspects that are considered desirable. For example, the norm might be to say that the government should aim to achieve x% economic growth or y% inflation.

Behavioral economics has also been accused of being the norm, since cognitive psychology is used to guide ("nudge") people to make the decisions they want by creating a structure for their choices.

Just as positive economics describes economic plans, situations, and conditions, normative economics seeks to prescribe solutions. Regulatory economic statements are used to identify and recommend ways to change economic policy or influence economic decision-making.

Normative economics and positive economics

Normative economics can help build and generate new ideas from multiple perspectives. But it cannot be the sole basis for making decisions on important economic issues because it does not use an objective perspective that focuses on facts and cause and effect relationships.

Economic statements coming from a positive economic perspective can be broken down into identifiable and observable facts that can be studied and verified. Because of this characteristic, economists, and analysts often practice their profession from a positive economic perspective. A positive economy serves as a measurable perspective that helps policymakers and other governments and businesses decide what matters to influence specific policies based on fact-based conclusions.

However, politicians (policymakers), business owners, and other organizations also typically consider what is desirable and undesirable for their respective components, turning normative economics into an equation while addressing significant economic issues, significant parts. When combined with positive economics, normative economics can produce a range of opinion-based solutions that reflect how individuals or entire communities view particular economic projects. These points of view are especially important for politicians (policymakers) or national leaders.

An example of normative economics

An example of a normative economy is:" We should have taxes to raise disposable income." In contrast, a positive or objective economic observation is:" Based on past data, a significant tax cut would help many people, but government budget constraints make this option unfeasible.". This particular judgment suggests that the level of disposable income should be increased.

Economic claims that are normative cannot be tested or proven for actual value or legitimate causality. Examples of normative economic statements include" Women should receive higher school loans than men"," Workers should receive more capitalist profits", and" Working citizens should not pay for hospital treatment". Normative economic statements often contain keywords such as "should" and "ought".

www.ingramcontent.com/pod-product-compliance
Lightning Source LLC
LaVergne TN
LVHW012016060526
838201LV00061B/4331